OUR

EVOLUTION

WALDO VIEIRA, M. D.

OUR

EVOLUTION

Rio de Janeiro, RJ - Brazil

INTERNATIONAL INSTITUTE OF PROJECTIOLOGY
AND CONSCIENTIOLOGY

1999

Notes:

– The author's rights to this edition have been graciously transferred by the author to the International Institute of Projectiology and Conscientiology (IIPC).
– The original pages of this edition were produced and revised using electronic desktop publishing and laser printing (text in Baskerville BE Regular; 245326 characters; 40769 words; 2391 sentences and 2623 paragraphs).

Translation: Andrea Santos

Proofreading: Álvaro Salgado, Cristina Arakaki, David Lindsay, Kevin de La Tour and Kim McCaul.

Cover: Fernando Santos

Printing and binding: OESP Gráfica S.A.

Card Catalog information prepared by the International Institute of Projectiology and Conscientiology (IIPC) Center of Information and Documentation

Vieira, Waldo, 1932 -

V658o   Our Evolution / Waldo Vieira. -
              1st Edition in English – Rio de Janeiro: International Institute of
              Projectiology and Conscientiology, 1999.
184 p.

              1. Conscientiology.   2. Projectiology.   I. Title

ISBN: 85-8619-42-9

                                                             CDD   133

IIPC - Instituto Internacional de Projeciologia e Conscienciologia
International Institute of Projectiology and Conscientiology (IIPC)
Rua Visconde de Pirajá, 572 / 6° andar - Ipanema - Rio de Janeiro - RJ - Brazil - CEP 22410-002
Tel.: 55-21-512-9229 Fax: 55-21-512-4735
Mailing Address: C.P. 70.000 - Rio de Janeiro - RJ - Brazil - CEP 22422-970
E-mail: iipc@iipc.org.br – Internet: http://www.iipc.org

TABLE OF CONTENTS

1. WHO ARE YOU?

Who are you?

What are you?

Where did you come from?

What are you doing in this life on Earth?

Where are you going?

We will give simple and logical responses to these five classic philosophical questions, as well as many others, from the standpoint of conscientiology, using a series of questions and answers.

What is *conscientiology?*

Conscientiology is the science that studies the "entire" consciousness (spirit, soul, ego), along with all of its bodies, existences, experiences, epochs and places, with an integral, projective, and self-aware approach in relation to the various existential dimensions.

I am a consciousness. You are a consciousness. All those who are near or far in human life and all self-aware beings in dimensions beyond human life are also consciousnesses.

OUR KNOWLEDGE IS ALWAYS INCREASING THROUGH OUR ACTIONS, AT ANY TIME AND PLACE WE MANIFEST OURSELVES.

Conscientiology invites you to undertake the following actions that are important for evolution: the optimization of your consciential (personal) progress; the manifestation of rational emotions and sentiments; the combating of self-corruption; the transformation of your personality into a catalyzing agent for the evolution of others; the understanding of the indestructibility of the consciousness; the rational organization of your own ideas; increased originality in your personal work; the attainment of a maximum level of de-repression. (removal) achievement

Through questions, answers, examples and emphatic phrases, this book will illustrate practical and more widely accepted conclusions – reached through lucid projectiology experiments – regarding the acts and manifestations of consciousnesses: you, me, and all those personalities who are more attentive to evolution.

What is *projectiology?*

Projectiology is the science that studies projections of the consciousness – lucid departures from the human body – and their effects. It includes projections of *consciential energies* beyond the *limits of the consciousness.*

To temporarily leave the human body with lucidity (out-of-body experience) is the most precious and practical source of clarification and consequential information on the most important issues of life, elucidating for us who we are, where we came from and where we are going.

Conscious human projection – currently achieved and experienced by millions of people – is a fact unknown to *Modern Philosophy.*

Conscious projection is directly achieved by the interested person, without any intermediaries. It is not experienced as a result of *merely hearing about it.*

We all leave our human body even if without lucidity. This is an unavoidable fact.

ANYONE CAN TEMPORARILY LEAVE THE PHYSICAL BODY WITH LUCIDITY. WILLFUL DESIRE AND THE USE OF SPECIFIC TECHNIQUES ARE SUFFICIENT TO ACHIEVE THIS RESULT.

Projective (OBE) techniques have *worked well* for millions of people, especially during the last three decades. They will not fail you.

The following are some examples of *transcendent phenomena* researched in projectiology: lucid projection; bilocation; remote viewing (traveling clairvoyance); internal viewing; nonalignment of the physical and non-physical bodies while in the waking state; double (compound) projection.

Everything we study here involves what you and I are doing at every moment according to leading-edge relative truths.

What is *leading-edge relative truth?*

A leading-edge relative truth is a new, more important reality that is worth being studied, discussed and placed ahead of others in the same area of research, to eventually be refuted as well.

The objective, in our case, is to indicate those evolutionary *courses of action* that are well *resolved* as well as those that are *poorly resolved* for the majority of consciousnesses at our current average level of evolution.

The interested individual will observe that we do not defend such leading-edge relative truths as either *cure-alls*, universal panaceas, or as absolute principles to live by.

Nor do we present ourselves in the irrational condition of having a monopoly on truth.

There are no absolute truths. Everything tends to evolve.

There are false truths in imposed ideas and all dogmas.

Dissidence is a part of all human endeavor. The majority of leading-edge relative truths arise from distilling discordant opinions.

IT IS CURRENTLY RATIONALLY INADMISSIBLE FOR ANYONE TO LIVE UNDER THE ENSLAVING CONTROL OF ANY DOGMA OR IMPOSED IDEA.

Nevertheless, millions of unwary people still live enslaved by the erroneous opinions of others.

It is far from our interest to convince anyone of anything. Even further to convince anyone of personal and group experiences. And further still to impose such experiences on excessively restricted individuals who do not wish personal renovation and feel comfortably fulfilled in the life that they lead.

Our intention is to provide critical knowledge regarding the dynamics of the evolution of the consciousness that is of interest to all, and to do this in an impartial and impersonal manner.

The conscientious researcher (or the researcher without preconceived ideas) will then confirm or refute these affirmations.

You alone will disagree or agree with the ideas presented here and you will either apply them in your daily life or discard them once and for all.

The most intelligent thing to do is to establish and maintain a natural healthy distance from any kind of *repression* (conditioning or limiting ideas), *sanctification* (considering anything as divine), and blind veneration or *brainwashing* with regards to people, ideas, institutions, objects, places or communities.

AS WE ALL KNOW, *PAPER* **ACCEPTS** **EVERYTHING THAT IS WRITTEN ON IT.** **A** *MICROPHONE* **WILL REGISTER** **ANY SOUND.**

It is more intelligent for us to maintain the greatest possible level of experiential discernment. We will only survive by acting with a maximum of lucidity within human society.

What is *human society?*

Human or intraphysical society is the set of all human beings, when gathered together to live as citizens of a country, or even as a planetary population.

Unfortunately, all of human society is still very sick.

We live in a hospital of immense proportions. This realization regarding the naked reality of our daily existence is, however, no excuse for discouragement or pessimism.

MILLIONS OF PEOPLE COMPOSE THE UNTHINKING HUMAN MASSES: THEY DO NOT THINK FOR THEMSELVES AND ARE SLAVES TO THE OPINIONS OF OTHERS.

Billions of *people*, victims of mental laziness, are *slaves* to individuals who judge themselves to be *opinion shapers* but deceitfully present themselves in the most diverse areas of intraphysical interest and work.

Human society everywhere is based upon the widespread manipulation of people by their leaders.

The best course of action is to avoid manipulating anyone and to avoid submitting to consciential manipulation.

Ideally, one will read these pages in a deeply contemplative manner, questioning everything with discernment and maturity.

In the first place, determine if there is sound reasoning in this text.

The personal discernment required in critical study to arrive at original libertarian ideas is worthwhile.

Above all, reflect upon the following primary affirmation and challenge: */if you think self-knowledge demands a great deal of effort, try to evolve with ignorance./*

2. Before the Human Body

What is the *holosoma?*

The holosoma is the set of all of the consciousness' bodies: the human, energetic, emotional and mental bodies.

We use different bodies in specific existential dimensions. In *physical life*, we use the human body.

In *non-physical life*, when we are projected outside the body, or during the intermissive period between lives, we use the emotional body (psychosoma, astral body) or the mental body (mentalsoma).

What is the *intermissive period?*

The intermissive period is the period of non-physical life or extraphysical interlude between our previous human life and the current one. It is also the period of non-physical life that we will have between the current human life and our next one.

In other words, there is an intermission *before* we acquire a *new* human body and another *after* we leave behind a *used, discarded* human body.

There are extraphysical periods in which the consciousness has greater or lesser degrees of lucidity (awareness).

In the intermissive period, we do not have a human body. We live, therefore, in a non-physical plane, or *extra*physical *dimension*, using a subtler body.

These non-physical or extraphysical dimensions have *communities* made up of consciousnesses who are also without physical bodies. Such consciousnesses form *extraphysical populations* on this planet, which greatly exceed the total human population in size.

THROUGH PROJECTIONS OF THE CONSCIOUSNESS, WE CAN ESTIMATE THAT THERE ARE 9 TIMES AS MANY EXTRAPHYSICAL CONSCIOUSNESSES AS THERE ARE HUMAN CONSCIOUSNESSES ON PLANET EARTH.

Conscious projectors, or those who temporarily leave their physical body with lucidity, provide consistently similar accounts of their visits to extraphysical communities.

In these extraphysical communities we realize that each one of us belongs to a specific evolutionary group.

What is an *evolutionary group?*

An evolutionary group is a gathering of more or less lucid consciousnesses who evolve together according to the affinity of their emotions, ideas and actions. It is the same as *karmic group* with respect to the law of cause and effect. Consciousnesses form *consciential families.*

EACH ONE OF US REFLECTS OTHER SIMILAR BEINGS WHO, IN TURN, MAINTAIN DEEP AFFINITIES WITH US.

Each consciousness has their own evolutionary group.

This group is composed of *millions of consciousnesses* in constant growth, existing in different evolutionary levels and dimensions.

Thousands of evolutionary *groups* compose the physical and extraphysical populations of planet earth.

The following are examples of *smaller groups* within our evolutionary group: the nuclear family (mother, father, siblings); the extended family (spouse, children and in-laws); the circle of our professional relations; the circle of our social relations in a club or a school; all the *leashes of the ego* that bind us within a society.

Doctrinaire groups, sectarian fraternities, labor unions and cooperative associations act as leashes of the ego.

When we are lucid during the intermissive period we establish our future projects with relative freedom.

These projects include the preliminary plans for one's *upcoming human life.*

All these projects depend on the considerations of our evolutionary group's Evolutionologist.

What is an *Evolutionologist?*

An Evolutionologist is a consciousness who has evolved beyond the average level of our evolutionary group. This consciousness has a broad, universalistic, integrated and ideal perception of each one's progress. The Evolutionologist is a specialist in the evolution or progress of consciousnesses.

Hundreds of Evolutionologists exist within each evolutionary group.

The more we dedicate ourselves to performing *clarifying assistance* in favor of other consciousnesses, the more minutely studied will be the programming of our next human life. In this context, we sometimes operate as a small brick within an enormous evolutionary construction.

The more we work in favor of the clarification of others, the greater will be our *freedom of action* within our evolutionary group.

It is important to reflect upon the fact that the act of *clarifying others* is more difficult and much less pleasing than the act of *consoling others.* Nevertheless, the act of clarifying others is evolutionarily more productive for all of us.

In general, it is very common for people to react instinctively against the truth that concerns them. This is the result of the natural, genetic, atavistic and animal instinct for survival.

When we demonstrate personal, assistantial, maxifraternal merit in the extraphysical dimensions, we are selected to participate in some type of intermissive course.

What is the *intermissive course?*

The intermissive course is a period of *specialized learning* that the more mature and deserving extraphysical consciousnesses undergo during the intermissive period.

THE INTERMISSIVE COURSE IS THE EXTRAPHYSICAL PREPARATION FOR CONSCIENTIAL REBIRTH INTO HUMAN LIFE.

In these intermissive courses, extraphysical consciousnesses, along with other students, attend classes, follow curriculums, undergo training and carry out residencies in research groups, some of which involve observation of the human dimension.

Students of advanced intermissive courses are accompanied to other planets on *extraphysical learning excursions.*

Veteran conscious projectors, while projected, are able to sporadically attend and retake some evolutionary extraphysical courses as *auditing students.*

There are very sophisticated intermissive courses that focus on the most diverse topics or disciplines.

There are subtle and unimaginable extraphysical instruments of study and investigation. For example, there are exact replicas of scenarios or live mock-ups of human environments where the extraphysical consciousnesses will soon live as intraterrestrial social beings, just like us.

Intermissive courses serve to accelerate, quicken or supercharge the evolution of consciousnesses.

They teach the students how to eliminate the repetition of useless acts.

They awaken in consciousnesses the rational intention and healthy desire to help their fellow beings.

They insightfully weave the planning of one human life with another within a logical chain of events in time and dimensions.

In short, intermissive courses help consciousnesses to improve their evolutionary performance in all aspects.

THERE ARE VETERAN TEACHERS OF INTERMISSIVE COURSES LIVING AMONG US.

Bearing in mind the ideas covered so far, ask yourself the following question:

Do you think you are at an advanced, average or inferior level within your evolutionary group?

No one should be reluctant to confront themselves with realistic self-analysis, regarding the most important aspects of life.

It is worth remembering that a coward is one of the sickest individuals in human life.

THE INTRAPHYSICAL CONSCIOUSNESSES (MEN AND WOMEN) WHO EVOLVE THE MOST ARE THOSE WHO CAN SEE WITH THE PARA-EYES OF THE PSYCHOSOMA.

The psychosoma is the emotional parabody (non-physical body) that we use in the majority of our conscious and unconscious projections.

3. DEACTIVATION OF THE ENERGETIC BODY

What is the *energetic body?*

The energetic body is the set of consciential energies that binds the emotional body to the human body. It is also called the *holochakra*, in reference to its energy centers.

Individuals may have a greater or lesser *flexibility* in the use of their energetic body.

Imbalances and blockages in the energetic body's consciential energies cause *disturbances and diseases* in the human body.

Those who are *better able to control* their consciential energies *suffer less from* illness.

PEOPLE CAN SUFFER AILMENTS AS THE RESULT OF A LACK AS WELL AS AN EXCESS OF CONSCIENTIAL ENERGIES.

The healthy balance of a person's consciential energies depends on what that person thinks, feels and does. In other words, it depends on the person's will and most profound intention.

The energetic body and our consciential energies manifest themselves with greater vigor in the *energetic dimension,* which acts intensely on the earth's paratroposphere.

The best resource for developing control and better use of our consciential energies is the vibrational state.

What is the *vibrational state?*

The vibrational state or VS is the technical condition of the maximum acceleration of the energies of the energetic body, through the impulsion of one's will.

The VS helps the practitioner to identify his or her own parapsychic signaletics.

What is *parapsychic signaletics?*

Parapsychic signaletics is the existence, identification and self-aware use of energetic, animic, parapsychic and extremely personal signals that everyone has. These signals are evidenced once the individual endeavors to perceive them.

ALL THE CONSCIENTIAL ENERGIES THAT WE USE ARE DERIVED FROM IMMANENT ENERGY, WHICH IS PRESENT EVERYWHERE.

What is *immanent energy?*

Immanent energy or IE is primary, vibrational, essential, multiform, impersonal energy, which is diffused throughout all objects in the universe in an omnipresent fashion.

IE is still untamed by the human consciousness. It is far too subtle to be detected by the physical instruments currently employed by modern technology.

To evolve is to absorb, discriminate, circulate, transfer, capture, transform, modulate, disperse, accumulate, recompose, emit and project consciential energy with ever increasing levels of lucidity. In this way, immanent energy will be completely controlled and used with greater intelligence.

The consciential energies of the energetic body make two connections: the most important one to the emotional body and the other to the human body. This maintains *matter* in an *energized* form and human life itself.

The consciousness, at our current level of evolution, neither *incarnates* nor binds directly to matter.

What occurs is simply a *direct energetic existence.* Or an *indirect consciential existence.*

What is the *first death?*

The first death is the *death of the human body* (soma), which severs the energetic connections with the emotional body. At that point, the connections binding the consciousness to dense, physical and biological matter are ruptured.

The death of the human body in a nuclear explosion, with its instantaneous dissipation, is the most impacting to the consciousness. Such an event forces the consciousness to undergo a lightning fast change from one consciential vehicle and existential dimension to another.

Helpers cooperate with and sponsor the occurrence of the first death in the case of specific deserving individuals.

Who is a *helper?*

A helper is a technical, assistantial, extraphysical consciousness who has a great affinity with the human consciousness being *assisted.*

Not everyone benefits from the assistance of a helper: only the micro-minority of individuals who have already given up their own *mega ego.*

ONLY A FEW INDIVIDUALS WHO WORK HARD IN FAVOR OF OTHERS HAVE MORE THAN ONE EXTRAPHYSICAL HELPER.

The human body is the most fragile and transitory of all of the consciousness' bodies. It decays or is deactivated more quickly than any of the other bodies.

Physical death is a liberation of energies.

Matter is a secondary derivative of energy. Energy and matter are, therefore, the same thing.

The human body is energized or vitalized organic matter. Besides energy and matter, there exists the consciousness.

What is *the consciousness?*

The consciousness is our greatest reality, it is what we are, beyond energy and matter.

The consciousness can be observed and analyzed both in the intraphysical and extraphysical states.

What is an *intraphysical consciousness?*

An intraphysical or human consciousness is what you and I are, while temporarily immersed in vitalized or energized matter.

What is an *extraphysical consciousness?*

An extraphysical consciousness is the paracitizen of the Extraphysical Society.

Energy binds the consciousness to matter.

Neither you nor I are the human body. The human body is an instrument that lasts a very short time. Like all matter, it is fleeting, mutable and recyclable.

The principle of energy conservation is also valid in this case: energy can not be created or destroyed, it can only be transformed.

WE CONSTANTLY DONATE AND ABSORB CONSCIENTIAL ENERGIES, USUALLY WITHOUT ANY AWARENESS.

Only a small minority of more conscious people absorbs or exteriorizes consciential energies whenever they wish.

Many aspects concerning the soma's death are still obscure. Research on thanatological phenomena is of great value.

What is the *second death?*

The second death is the liberation of *residual* human consciential *energies* that remain attached to the emotional body after the person has passed away. This evidences the existence of *residual* or clinging *consciential energies* that are not easily discarded due to the consciousness' attachment to physical matter.

The second death drains the consciousness' *remnant vital energy.* In the case of less ill consciousnesses, the second death generally occurs three days after the individual's first death.

ALL STUDENTS OF INTERMISSIVE COURSES HAVE OBVIOUSLY ALREADY UNDERGONE THE TRANSITION OF THE SECOND DEATH.

This means that the second death is a pre-requisite for taking intermissive courses and that the course candidates have already totally and definitively freed themselves from the energies of the energetic body of their most recent human life.

These *clean* extraphysical consciousnesses, upon undergoing the second death, no longer have any of the *biological energies,* which were discarded with the death of the human body.

The first death is the *first depuration* of the consciousness' energies. The second death, is the *second depuration* of energies.

The refinement or dissipation of these two types of energies brings consciousnesses closer to their *true reality.*

In this way, consciousnesses reach a freer and lighter state, enjoying the full extent of their own *depurated* emotional body.

Now free from any direct influences of dense matter, extraphysical consciousnesses get farther and farther away from the earth's troposphere and thus more distant from their own personal, material, animal, parochial problems or from their *own little world.*

This situation greatly influences the betterment of consciousnesses, especially with regards to their conscientization (self-awareness), evolutionary reality and intelligent projects for the immediate future.

The second death, therefore, constitutes a maximal sympathetic de-assimilation of the extraphysical consciousness' energies.

What is *sympathetic de-assimilation?*

Sympathetic de-assimilation is the willful discharging of residual, *undesirable* or sick consciential energies that entered and lingered, even if temporarily, within our consciential micro-universe.

Strictly speaking, sympathetic de-assimilation is a therapeutic, self-healing process of balancing and unblocking of consciential energies, for the purpose of leaving *consciousnesses* healthy and *depurated,* with only their own personal energies.

TEAMS OF EVOLUTIONOLOGISTS HELP EXTRAPHYSICAL CONSCIOUSNESSES PASS THROUGH THE TRANSITION OF THE SECOND DEATH.

Just as the helper assists the *human consciousness* to temporarily leave the human body in the case of a conscious projection, or definitively leave the body, in the case of the first death, so does the Evolutionologist assist the *extraphysical consciousness* to discard the energetic body in the transition of the second death.

At this point, the following question is appropriate:

Has that dear relative of yours, who passed away so long ago and whom you have never forgotten, already gone through the second death?

This is a very practical question.

If you constantly evoke or call upon a deceased relative

who has not gone through the second death, he or she can affect you with sick consciential energies, even unknowingly or unconsciously, simply moved by affinity and emotions.

This constitutes a common type of interconsciential intrusion, causing mental and even physical illnesses.

Extraphysical intruders find their best supporters in human life among those who are interested in or foment wars.

4. Extraphysical Hometown

What is our *extraphysical hometown?*

Our extraphysical hometown is the non-physical community that each of us left when we acquired our current human body and that we will each return to once our human body is deactivated.

Our life in this human dimension is, obviously, always brief.

Our relationships with one another in this material existence are always precarious and transitory.

The extraphysical hometown is our true origin as consciousnesses; it is the exact personal dimension of each human consciousness, our native community.

In the same way that a Human or Intraphysical Society exists, so does an Extraphysical Society exist.

As citizens of the cosmos, we always belong to the Extraphysical Society we came from.

Our extraphysical hometown is the *district* where we come from and to which we will shortly and inevitably return. It is our *permanent residence* as consciousnesses in evolution.

Our *extraphysical roots* come first and prevail over our current human roots. They go beyond our citizenship and our human identity. It will always be like that, after this life and the deactivation of our human body.

All this implies three logical questions:

Where were you two years before being reborn into your current human body?

What is your fundamental evolutionary group?

Who are your evolutionary companions and best friends?

Our most intimate circle of friends is not solely composed of the personalities in our human family.

It is sufficient to recall the supposition that for each intraphysical consciousness there exist 9 extraphysical consciousnesses, in order to conclude that we are aware of only a few components of our evolutionary group while in this human life.

Extraphysical experiences demonstrate that we live, in our current evolutionary condition, to serve and mutually assist each other.

What is *assistantial intercession?*

Assistantial intercession is the provision of mutual help between people or lucid consciousnesses.

Assistantial intercessions in favor of needy consciousnesses in the extraphysical dimensions are extremely intense. This is particularly the case in the extraphysical dimensions that are near the earth's crust or troposphere.

What is the *troposphere?*

The troposphere is the atmospheric layer that extends from sea level to an average altitude of 6.35 miles (10 kilometers).

The earth's crust is the portion of this planet's troposphere where we find our evolutionary group's most primitive, needy and disturbed consciousnesses, both in the intraphysical and the corresponding extraphysical dimension.

IT IS EASIER FOR LUCID CONSCIOUSNESSES TO CONTACT EACH OTHER EXTRAPHYSICALLY THAN TO MAKE COMMON, PHYSICAL HUMAN CONTACT.

Thought is the true vehicle of transportation for the lucid consciousness.

The identification of the personal extraphysical hometown is more easily achieved through conscious projections and retrocognitions.

What is *retrocognition?*

Retrocognition is the lucid recollection of past experiences. In this case, it is the recollection of experiences prior to the individual's human rebirth.

INTERMISSIVE RETROCOGNITIONS CAN INCLUDE MEMORIES OF THE INTERMISSIVE COURSE OR THE INNATE IDEAS OF THE RETROCOGNITOR.

What are *innate ideas?*

Innate ideas are those ideas that the person is born with. They rationally explain the existence of *precocious children* or infant prodigies in the fields of science, the arts and human abilities in general.

We are all born *knowing something* that goes beyond our genetic inheritance.

What is *genetics?*

Genetics is the area of biology that studies the laws of transmission of hereditary characteristics and the properties of the elements that ensure this transmission.

Innate ideas are contained in our *integral memory*, which is multimillenary. This 'archive' is much ampler than the more restricted cerebral memory.

Our innate ideas existed before this human life. They will continue with us after the death of our brain. They will be with us in our next physical life and in our next human brain.

Innate ideas are predominantly acquired in the intermissive period, especially through intermissive courses.

In the same way that the *recent **cerebral** memory* of the physically mature person is the most difficult to retain, so is the *recent **integral** memory* of the consciousness the most difficult to access.

It is less difficult to have retrocognitions of previous lives from *two **thousand** years ago* than to remember what we were doing *two **years** before* acquiring this human body.

THE PERSONAL PATRIMONY OR THE ACTIVE LEGACY OF EVOLVED INNATE IDEAS VARIES FROM PERSON TO PERSON.

Innate ideas help human consciousnesses to remember their extraphysical hometown.

Having covered these concepts, a personal question is appropriate:

Have you stopped to reflect on the quality and useful application of your innate ideas?

Our performance, potentialities, and personal vocations are dependent upon our innate ideas.

5. HUMAN REBIRTH

Human or intraphysical rebirth is the activation of *a new energetic body*, which emanates from the psychosoma of the extraphysical consciousness. It raises several questions concerning our family.

Why were you born from your mother and not from any other woman?

This happened because there is a *law of affinity* or of relationships between consciousnesses. This law applies to both human and extraphysical consciousnesses.

Consciousnesses are attracted by their most profound affinities.

Many cases of expecting women who die from a *complicated labor* are due to insufficient affinity – or *sheer antagonism* – between the consciousness of the fetus and the consciousness of the pregnant woman.

The majority of *smooth pregnancies and easy labors* are due to a profound affinity – *or great empathy* – between the consciousness of the fetus and the consciousness of the mother.

A complicated pregnancy and labor signify a *lesser* energetic affinity between the *consciousness-mother* and the extraphysical consciousness in the rebirth process.

OUR PREVIOUS EXTRAPHYSICAL RELATIONSHIPS DETERMINE THE RELATIVE HEALTH OF OUR CURRENT HUMAN RELATIONSHIPS

Our destiny, in material existence, is determined during our most recent extraphysical past by the Evolutionologist of our evolutionary group.

Contact through the extraphysical and physical dimensions between the child-to-be and the parents-to-be can occur over a period of just a few days or over a long period of time before conception.

Human life is essentially an energetic connection.

The existential energetic connection occurs *within* the holosoma of the future child, *within* the bonds of the future parents and relatives, and especially *within* the holosoma of the future mother.

The connection between the energetic body and matter *most frequently occurs at the exact moment of human conception.* This is the most common point at which the consciousness reconnects to organic matter. During intraphysical life, a woman produces nearly 400 ova.

In most instances of rebirth, the spermatozoid's entry into the ovum marks the formal beginning of the human body's life.

What is *Embryology?*

Embryology is the science that studies the formation and development of the embryo.

What is an *embryo?*

An embryo is an organism, in this case human, which is in its first stages of development, or rather, is within the first 8 weeks of intrauterine life.

The embryo is not the consciousness.

The consciousness does not have *direct contact* with organic matter.

Energy serves as the intermediary between the consciousness and matter.

Every human life is indirectly developed through the energetic body. That is why any consciousness in a human body can leave or project themselves with lucidity to other dimensions, beyond dense material life.

THE INTRAPHYSICAL CONSCIOUSNESS LIVES IMPRISONED, IN AN INDIRECT FASHION, INSIDE THE HUMAN BODY, LIKE A CAPTIVE BALLOON.

This explains the development of the inevitable and useful phenomenon of conscious projection by everyone, without exception.

Some consciousnesses remain *indocile*, ready to leave the body.

To project every night while sleeping, even if unconsciously, is just like breathing for the human consciousness: it is a permanent, unchangeable and indispensable function of our consciential structure.

NO ONE RECEIVES A SPECIFIC MOTHER AND FATHER BY CHANCE. THERE ARE PROFOUND BONDS BETWEEN CONSCIOUSNESSES WHO EVOLVE TOGETHER.

In the majority of cases of physical rebirth, the mutual experiences of a more intimate or less intimate life together come from sharing many human lives over many centuries.

The more evolved the consciousness preparing itself to be reborn, the longer will be the extraphysical period of adaptation to dense matter and the preparation for living in the environment of the future parents before the moment of conception.

There are children-to-be who know and closely follow, in the unique condition of helpers, the two *single individuals* who will become their parents and who have not yet physically met each other.

On the other hand, there are many cases of affective lack and emotional disturbance wherein the extraphysical consciousnesses predisposed to a new human life operate as *conscious intruders* of their future parents.

In many cases, the animal conception of a new human life is the healthiest way to relieve the multiple conflicts and emotional disturbances within a group of intraphysical and/or extraphysical consciousnesses.

Even before becoming pregnant, veteran conscious female projectors are able to identify and monitor the characteristic details of the future human life that will come into existence through them.

Many women, during their pregnancy, are able to have conscious projections together with the consciousness of their future child, who is also projected.

What is *intraphysical restriction?*

INTRAPHYSICAL RESTRICTION IS THE FUNNELLING EFFECT OF PERSONAL ATTRIBUTES IMPOSED ON THE CONSCIOUSNESS WHO IS REBORN ON EARTH.

Every extraphysical consciousness temporarily loses many of their talents, personal evolutionary conquests and knowledge when they acquire a new human body.

Consciousnesses lose the overwhelming majority of their *units of lucidity* at the moment of conception and recuperate whatever potentialities they can during their material life.

The recuperation of the consciousness' *integrally lucid personality* occurs little by little from childhood up through physical maturity.

Rarely, however, does a person exhibit and employ 80% of the lucidity and discernment that they possessed as an extraphysical consciousness.

In human life, we lose the brilliance and the splendor of the lucidity that we enjoyed in our previous extraphysical life.

While inside a soma, we are always incomplete personalities in comparison to our personal, maximum, multimillenary attributes.

As human beings we typically employ only 1 or, in the case of some *notable personalities in history,* 3 of our countless intelligences.

We are not able to access all the memories contained in our *integral memory.* Is the brain too limited to support the integral accounts of our parabrain or are we simply not able to exercise it efficiently?

What is the *parabrain?*

It is the brain of our extraphysical emotional body or psychosoma. It is also the seat of our extraphysical mental body, or vehicle of discernment.

The brain of our new body does not reflect the consciential expansion that we freely enjoyed in the extraphysical dimension – our true origin.

In summary, at our current evolutionary level, to live in dense matter is to reduce ourselves to an insignificant fraction of our inner reality.

In other words, our *consciential micro-universe* becomes even *more reduced* in human life.

Despite all this, we must not forget that a small expansion (development or an increase in number) of our *specific* consciential attributes can be obtained in each human life.

At our current evolutionary level, physical life is still much more productive for all of us than extraphysical life because it is more difficult to fulfill our need for interconsciential assistance in the extraphysical dimension. Assistance is an irreplaceable component in the leveraging of personal and group evolution.

THE *40* WEEKS OF INTRAUTERINE LIFE IS THE MOST RESTRICTED PHYSICAL PERIOD FOR THE REBORN CONSCIOUSNESS.

Beyond genetics, the science that studies the laws of transmission of inherited characteristics of individuals, there is paragenetics.

What is *paragenetics?*

Paragenetics pertains to the genetic inheritance of the consciousness, through the emotional body, from the existence prior to the human embryo.

The more evolved the consciousness in the process of human rebirth, the *smaller* are the influences of genetics and the *greater* are the influences of paragenetics on the embryo, the fetus and the life within the mother's uterus.

It is for this reason that the *degree of restriction* that is suffered by the consciential micro-universe during intrauterine life varies greatly from consciousness to consciousness.

Human consciousnesses inherit much more paragenetically from themselves than they inherit genetically from their parents.

Besides the powerful determining factor of genetics (*an inheritance from one's parents*) and paragenetics (*an inheritance from oneself*), there is another type of permanent influence over the new human body of the reborn consciousness: Ecology.

What is *Ecology?*

Ecology is the part of biology that studies the relationships between living beings and their environment, as well as their reciprocal influences.

A third order of influence results, therefore, from Ecology – *an inheritance from the human environment*, the social, cultural inheritance or from the milieu where the person is raised, studies, physically develops and lives until maturity.

We are, therefore, the result of a set of three inheritances: from our parents (genetics), from ourselves (paragenetics) and from the human, social and cultural environment (Ecology).

In our evolutionary self-analysis, our genetic inheritance should be considered first.

It is important to remember that we all – human beings of all races without exception – have a caudal appendage, that is a tail, until the 10th week of intrauterine life.

In addition, we still have 4 *canine teeth*, two in the upper jaw and two in the lower jaw just like many subhuman carnivores, especially the dog, *man's best friend.*

We also know today that 96.7% of our genetic composition is identical to that of the chimpanzee.

HUMANS STILL EXHIBIT SOME FORMS OF SUBHUMAN BEHAVIOR, WHICH ARE IDENTICAL TO THOSE OF CHIMPANZEES.

Nonetheless, we should not be ashamed of being human.

All healthy women, even those who are quite cultured, intellectual and finely educated, have pubic hair - signs of the female-animal. We all owe our intraphysical life to women.

It is extremely important to avoid traumas during pregnancy and labor in order to ensure the well being of the future adult human body and the mature life of the consciousness who is in the process of rebirth into matter.

The physical and mental hygiene of pregnant and parturient women is indispensable in order to prevent eclampsia, abortion, and other accidents that usually result from the shock of consciential energies between the consciousnesses of the future mother and the fetus (future newborn).

At this point, it is very important to pose a pertinent question:

Which of these three fundamental personal inheritances influences you the most?

The answer to this question synthesizes the value and the quality of your millenary past.

NO ONE ESCAPES FROM THEIR OWN PAST. THE PAST ONLY SERVES TO AVOID MAKING THE SAME MISTAKES AGAIN.

6. CHILDHOOD

What is *childhood?*

Childhood (infancy) is the period of growth in human beings that spans from birth to puberty.

Abstract thought is very difficult for children.

Contrary to the affirmations of conventional sciences – which only investigate *the consciousness in a superficial manner* – extraphysical research of evolutionary group processes shows that, in most cases, the consciousness is responsible for both the type and gender of the human body that is acquired.

Parents can be classified into two types: those who are traditional and rigid (outdated) and those who are modern and open, being better adapted to the renovations occurring in our current human era.

Biological laws govern intrauterine life. The belly of the modern mother is a very fragile protective cover for the fetus.

The formation of the human body of the consciousness in the rebirth process on earth is greatly affected by the negative habits of the parents, such as, ingestion of chemical substances, antibiotics, the sick habit of smoking, alcohol consumption, light and heavy drugs.

The *mother* plays a predominant role in human gestation. She has a *unique blood-to-blood connection* with the reborn consciousness.

The *father* always has a much more fragile bond with the fetus.

THE ENERGETIC, EMOTIONAL AND INTELLECTUAL ATMOSPHERE OF THE PARENTS STRONGLY INFLUENCES THE CONSCIOUSNESS DURING THE REBIRTH PROCESS.

The infant's life is always a *simple one.*

During childhood, the human consciousness is only able to shape the foundations of their soma.

What is the *soma?*

Soma is the technical name for the male and female human body. It is the *crudest* body of the physical consciousness, being an extension of the earth, although 65% of its mass is made up of water. At the same time, the human body is the *highest* known level of animal evolution.

EVERY SOMA IS CREATED THROUGH A HETEROSEXUAL ACT INVOLVING MUTUAL, PREDOMINANTLY ANIMAL STIMULUS.

We need to take constant care of our human body *without paranoia.*

For those of us currently in the intraphysical state, the human body, limited by our physical senses, is our most concrete, objective or least subtle personal component.

Due to its solid nature, the human body makes the common man and woman, devoid of any basic notions of multidimensionality, think that they are first and foremost their soma, and nothing more.

Men say: "my body" and by doing so, they separate their soma from the consciousness. Women say: "I" and by doing so they make an absolute psychological integration of their soma with the consciousness.

This myopic overestimation of the soma is characteristic of physicalist individuals who still lack the practical discernment afforded by consciential evolution.

There are people who do not have sufficient intelligence to prevent the putrefaction of their own soma while consciously living in it.

The soma is the *first coffin* of many users who are still alive in this human existence.

These people live a sedentary life, smoke, intoxicate themselves with excessive drink and drugs, and fail to reconcile their differences with their adversaries. This is a pathological condition which they somatize (internalize) and which eventually creates disturbances or diseases.

IT IS BETTER TO LIVE IN A CONDITION OF PERMANENT LOVE. DISAFFECTION AGES AND PREMATURELY KILLS THE HUMAN ORGANISM.

To live for the soma is insanity.

Under the skin of the most beautiful physical human form lies a skull.

The soma needs rest and cellular recomposition. The consciousness, on the other hand, never stops, nor does it need to rest simultaneously with the soma. This is why we can project ourselves into other consciential dimensions.

The following two questions apply:

*If you do not make good use of your **brain**, the noblest human organ, how do you expect to make good use of your entire human body?*

*If you do not make good use of your **human body**, the simplest of your bodies, how do you expect to make good use of all your other more complex vehicles of manifestation?*

Our house or apartment – legal address, residence – is the extension of the human body in this intraphysical life.

We keep our human body alive firstly through consciential energies and secondly by breathing oxygen with the lungs. There are also secondary factors that serve to keep the body alive, such as liquid and solid nourishment, hygiene, physical exercise, and others.

Our human body is a *bellows-body*.

As a result, we permanently and unavoidably live in this physical life as *animal respirators*.

We can not stop breathing for even 10 minutes; otherwise we definitively deactivate our instrument of communication.

From the day it is born, the mother, the pediatrician and those responsible for the newborn baby are concerned about its ability to breathe freely in an unpolluted environment.

Only those who have experienced high-level conscious projections can evaluate with experiential rationality, the *unavoidable burden* that is the body's incessant *respiratory mechanism*.

While *writing* these lines, the author's lungs – his *bellows of flesh* – worked without resting, very much the same way that while *reading* these lines, your *bellows of flesh* do not stop even for a second.

On the other hand, while utilizing the emotional body, the projected consciousness temporarily stops breathing. This *healthy loss of respiration* is a new sensation that the *great majority* of the human population has never experienced.

If you have not yet projected yourself outside your body with sufficient lucidity, you certainly can not evaluate the experience of being fully aware of not having to breathe.

IT IS ALWAYS RECOMMENDED THAT PEOPLE UNDERGO THE EXPERIENCE OF EXISTING WITHOUT BREATHING IN ORDER TO ACCELERATE THEIR EVOLUTION.

The average person immediately relates this subject to their phobias or to pathological issues, such as the horror of suffocation. For such individuals this possibility is irrational and they are incapable of considering it.

The **un**conscious projector is not yet capable of experiencing the healthy liberation afforded by the tranquility of not breathing.

Nonetheless, the human body is only the *skin* of the whole personality.

Unfortunately, Human Society generally only considers the human body in an immediatist and utilitarian manner. Little or no attention is paid to the energetic and emotional bodies, and the *entire* personality.

This is why there are so many people who erroneously think that they are composed solely of their body of flesh, and who end up living exclusively *for* and *through* the soma.

Obviously, this is not entirely *un*desirable. These people seek and maintain this condition. It is, therefore, a choice, which is to be respected.

Strictly speaking, we came into human life, at this evolutionary level, to be happy, cheerful and to do whatever we want, as long as we respect the human and consciential rights of others. This is, in fact, the underlying rule of conduct of the ancient hedonistic principles.

What is *hedonism?*

Hedonism is the doctrine that considers immediate and individual pleasure to be the only possible good, the beginning and the end of moral life.

On the other hand, we should not indulge in excesses. No one comes to human life solely to delight themselves in desserts, *the good life, fresh water, cool breezes*, laziness and sedentary life.

Prolonged physical inactivity kills the human body.

THE HUMAN BABY IS THE MOST DEFENSELESS OF ALL BABY ANIMALS ON EARTH.

The human child demands constant care and attention, especially during the first years of life.

The period between 2 and 5 years of age is critical in human childhood. It is a phase of nourishment for the mental body or of *acquisition of knowledge* that is fundamental for consciousnesses in their new vehicle of manifestation.

According to anthropological research, babies within this age range who are accidentally *raised by wolves* or bears are never able to become normal human adults.

What is *anthropology?*

Anthropology is a science composed of several disciplines whose common aim is to describe human beings and to analyze them based on the biological and cultural characteristics of the groups to which they belong. Emphasis is given to the differences and variations among these groups in different epochs.

During the first years of human life, the consciousness reborn onto this planet goes through the foolishness, ignorance and repetitions of the consciential basement.

What is the *consciential basement?*

The consciential basement is the phase of infantile manifestation that lasts up through the end of human puberty. During this phase, the reborn consciousness exhibits a strong prevalence of basic animal instincts, primitive appetites and the vigorous influence of their genetic heritage.

Everyone inevitably goes through the initial intraphysical stage of the consciential basement.

However, the characteristics and consequences of this period vary from person to person.

The vast majority of people present *neurotic infantile behavior* to one degree or another.

The consciential basement is the personality's *sewage department*, where one is *more a slave* and *less a master* of primitive impulses or the remnants of imperfections.

The most diverse personal *flaws*, often considered to be permanently buried in the consciousness' past, can *reappear* more intensely during the infantile period of the consciential basement.

The manifestation of the consciential basement is more clearly pronounced in *boys* than in girls. We all know that boys are more aggressive. Girls smile more often.

A classic example of the consciential basement is the destructive, opposing and antisocial behavior of children.

The extent of the consciential basement expresses the level of excellence of the consciousness' recent *intermissive course*, whether it was basic or advanced. This fact is more evident in the critical period from 2 to 5 years, the age of acquisition of *preliminary knowledge*.

Childhood is, in theory, the worst period of human life.

This can be rationally explained: while struggling with the new energies of the energetic body and the new human body we are unable to express our personal maturity or maximal discernment.

Above all, what matters the most for consciousnesses, regardless of the dimension where they manifest, is their level of lucidity.

The child's life is merely a practice run, a sketch, a project and a promise.

During this initial period, we are neither able to achieve proper conditions nor have an opportunity to fulfill any meaningful portion of a more advanced existential program with lucidity and dignity.

What is the *existential program?*

THE EXISTENTIAL PROGRAM IS THE SPECIFIC PROGRAMMING OF EACH HUMAN CONSCIOUSNESS IN THEIR NEW LIFE IN THIS PHYSICAL DIMENSION.

There are giving or *greater* existential programs, dedicated to the well being of many; and there are receiving or *lesser* existential programs dedicated to specific personal matters.

This is why it is very embarrassing to hear a mature person complain that their childhood was the best time of their life.

This complaint exalts the unfinished, one's frustrations and the worst. It shows that the person feels unfulfilled because they were not able to complete the greater tasks that they had planned to execute in the adult phase, the most important period of human life.

This happens even when consciousnesses do not really know in greater detail what they came to do in physical life, only *unconsciously* sensing and identifying the duty that they accepted.

At this point, it is useful to perform a self-analysis by answering two questions:

Were you a balanced or an unbalanced child?

Do you still regret the foolishness of your consciential basement?

For many people, the consciential basement persists through adolescence and even into maturity. When this happens, the person becomes a *maladjusted adult.*

Personal experience is the cornerstone of the consciousness' evolutionary life.

There is no intraphysical consciousness who is totally free. We live in a system of generalized interdependence between consciousnesses, all the time, everywhere.

It is hypothesized that very undisciplined intraphysical consciousnesses, or those who are difficult to interact and live with, had either a very short period as *domesticated animals* together with humans or none at all, during the multimillenary development of their consciential, multiexistential, subhuman, human or intraphysical evolution.

The subhuman animal, beyond its genetic pre-programming, learns to have some discipline through contact with humans.

This happens before *losing the caudal appendage* (tail).

Consciousnesses are more entropic and disorganized when they did not go through this period of prolonged relationship.

Thus, we can conclude that the details of evolutionary paths differ greatly from one consciousness to another because humans do not tame and domesticate *all* types of subhuman animals.

7. ADOLESCENCE

What is *adolescence?*

Adolescence is the period of human life that occurs after childhood. It begins with puberty and is characterized by a number of corporal, psychological or integral consciential changes. It lasts approximately from 12 to 20 years of age.

Adolescence is the phase of human life in which social values are acquired and projects are elaborated that result in the consciousness' integration into society, or adaptation to the current human life.

The adolescent phase is a familiar womb-like experience.

During adolescence, a trip programmed by physiological development, one's biological alarm clock goes off. Girls have their *menarche* or first menstruation. No modern woman will ever forget her first bra or her first menstruation.

In boys, physiological development explodes with the *semenarche*, or first ejaculation.

Genetic programming obeys an unavoidable biological determinism.

ADOLESCENTS ARE BIG CHILDREN: THEY LACK THE AVERAGE ADULT'S GREATER MATURITY.

This lack of maturity gives rise to the irregularities of puberty or the foolishness resulting from the *consciential basement* of the reborn consciousness, with respect to affective, sexual, educational and social life.

In adolescence, consciousnesses having a weaker personality are tempted to lazily accommodate themselves, through the law of least effort, to their readily available talents and all that they bring from the past – the baggage of previous life experiences. They thus surrender themselves as defenseless victims of existential self-mimicry.

What is *existential self-mimicry?*

Existential self-mimicry is the human consciousness' generally instinctive and unconscious imitation of their own past experiences or previous physical existences.

This complacency can annul a good portion of one's existential program that was planned before rebirth.

During adolescence, the *reborn* extraphysical consciousnesses, now in a new human body, be it female or male, begin to define or exuberantly define their *basic sexual instinct.*

This definition occurs based on the predominance of either paragenetics or genetics, relative to the will of the human consciousness.

Disturbances in the emotional body act powerfully in the definition of the basic sexual instinct.

SEX IS IN THE SOMA. SEXUAL MATURITY IS ONLY ACHIEVED THROUGH A CLEAR SELF-DEFINITION OF THE BASIC, PERSONAL SEXUAL INSTINCT.

Consciousnesses can, for example, receive a new, healthy, fully functioning male body and feel more comfortable using it in a displaced or ectopic female manner, in accordance with their basic sexual instinct.

What is *consciential ectopia?*

Consciential ectopia is the unsatisfactory execution of one's existential program in an eccentric, dislocated manner, outside the *programming* chosen for the individual's *intraphysical life.* This *eccentricity,* ectopia or deviation can begin through the inappropriate use of the human body.

This abnormal usage causes imbalance and blockages in one's chakras and gives rise to the greatest conflicts and maladjustments of human sexuality.

The great majority of parents still program the future of their children without giving any consideration to their existential programs.

What is a *chakra?*

A chakra is a nucleus or defined field of consciential energy in the energetic body of the consciousness, which is reflected in the human body.

What is the *sexchakra?*

The sexchakra is the nucleus of consciential energies acting as the main link between the energetic body and the human body. It is also called *radical* or root chakra (geoenergy).

It is located at the center of the perineum, both in men and women, with the energies directed mainly backwards and downwards.

CONSCIOUSNESSES DO NOT HAVE GENDER, PER SE. BEING THUS ASEXUAL, THEY CAN NOT REPRODUCE OTHER CONSCIOUSNESSES.

Within the set of bodies of the consciousness, only the human body has gender. That is why the human body, or soma, is also called the *sexsoma.*

However, the main sexual instrument is, in fact, the will. That is why we affirm: *somatic sex* is between the groins and *holosomatic sex* is between the ears.

We can see that the instinctive processes actively influence the utilization of the human body. These processes are the baggage that we inherit from ourselves and our ancestors.

Sex education is still developing everywhere. This has a great effect on the adolescent period.

The *sexual revolution* that involved recent human generations has placed individuals in the middle of three competing groups with regards to sex education: family, school and media.

Unfortunately, this can continue in a pathological manner.

The instinctive processes can remain with the consciousness of the deceased person during the intermissive period and reappear in the new physical life. This may occur once or in many successive lives.

A frank inner conflict is established when consciousnesses consider themselves to intrinsically and erroneously belong to a specific sexual gender and the new physical body they acquire is of the opposite gender. This explains the countless cases of homosexuality.

Many genetic, paragenetic and environmental factors influence and intensify even more this inner maladjustment of the consciousness.

Due to the complexity of these conflicts, they need to be individually analyzed according to conscientiotherapeutic norms.

What is *Conscientiotherapy?*

Conscientiotherapy is the area of conscientiology that studies and applies the treatment, alleviation and remission of disturbances of the consciousness. This is achieved by applying the resources and techniques offered by conscientiology.

Sex is extremely important for everyone's human or energetic life without exception.

Sexual-affective myths generate sexual identity crises.

SEX IS AT THE ROOT OF CONSCIENTIAL ENERGIES. IT IS ALSO THE MOST POPULAR PROFESSIONAL AND AMATEUR HUMAN SPORT EVERYWHERE.

The human being has the most developed sexuality of any animal on this planet.

Consciousnesses must adapt to their new existential period with the energies of the new energetic body in the new human body. The restriction experienced by consciousnesses while manifesting in matter imposes this forced adaptation.

The reborn consciousness, now *disguised* in a new body and within a new social context, is often discovered and identified by the extraphysical enemies from the past several lives, according to the laws of existential seriality.

What is *existential seriality?*

Existential seriality is the evolutionary process that imposes successive (in series) intraphysical rebirths.

It is easy to see that this intensifies the inner conflicts experienced during adolescence.

Sex, or more appropriately the affective-sexual condition, results in an indeterminate series of influences, hypnosis and sick intrusions between consciousnesses. This is the condition of interconsciential intrusion.

What is *interconsciential intrusion?*

INTERCONSCIENTIAL INTRUSION IS THE PATHOLOGICAL INVASION OR INTRUSION OF IDEAS, EMOTIONS AND ENERGIES OF ONE CONSCIOUSNESS UPON ANOTHER.

Intrusion can occur in 4 different ways: from an *extra*physical consciousness to another *extra*physical consciousness, from an *extra*physical consciousness to an *intra*physical consciousness; from an *intra*physical consciousness to another *intra*physical consciousness; and from one *intra*physical consciousness to an *extra*physical consciousness (rare).

Thus, both extraphysical interconsciential intrusion and human interconsciential intrusion exist.

Interconsciential intrusion is the most common illness or disturbance in human beings. It attacks our brains more often than cavities do our teeth. Its pathological effects are much worse, more prolonged and devastating than all other disturbances and pathologies.

Extraphysical intruders are like the shadow cast by the body of an intraphysical consciousness: they change position and alter their form according to the ambience (dimension) and temporal circumstance (moment).

Unfortunately, extraphysical intrusions potentiate organic illnesses or those specifically related to the soma.

One of the characteristics of intraphysical intruders is their *negative emotional inversion.*

We know that we use less energy, less effort and fewer muscles to smile than to make a sad or worried face.

When a person routinely maintains an unpleasant disposition, constantly frowning rather than smiling, it is a physical sign of obsession with some wearisome issue and pathological intrusion.

The consciousness is indestructible. Consequently, the worst that can happen as a result of consciential intrusion – the subjugation of one consciousness by another, or outright *pathological possession* – is the deactivation of the incautious intraphysical victim's human body.

No one can ever definitively deactivate the consciousness, not *sick-possessors,* not even the *sick-possessed,* and especially not *sick-suicide victims.*

Interconsciential intrusions are less likely to occur during childhood due to the still sketchy and incomplete brain development of the person who is still far from physical maturity.

Interconsciential intrusion is much more frequent at the end of adolescence at which point the reborn consciousness defines their sexual preference, company and mode of *reliving* in their new human life.

Remnant *viscous* consciential energies, that are responsible for blockages and imbalances in our energetic body, are the result of insufficient *sympathetic de-assimilation* from the energies of other consciousnesses, subhuman animals, plants, objects and environments. These energies establish prolonged or *chronic* interconsciential intrusions.

THOUSANDS OF PRODUCTIVE HUMAN LIVES HAVING PROMISING EXISTENTIAL PROGRAMS ARE RENDERED USELESS DUE TO INTERCONSCIENTIAL INTRUSION.

We can see that this all happens because people generally do not know how to perform *sympathetic de-assimilation* or *rid themselves of* the sick consciential energies that they absorbed after a pathological energetic contact. The sympathetic de-assimilation allows individuals to return to their original *clean* state.

This is why adolescence is a *defining crossroads* of human destiny for the reborn consciousness on earth.

The individual's vocational directives begin to appear during adolescence and thus the first indicators of his or her economic level, as well as the scope of his or her adult intellectual life.

The young projector's first initiatives with respect to the phenomena of *lucid projectability* start to surface during adolescence. A search for existential inversion also begins for those who had an advanced intermissive course.

What is *existential inversion?*

Existential inversion is a technique that inverts sociocultural values and projects in human life. This allows the execution of greater personal endeavors – that are usually performed during adulthood – to be commenced in one's youth.

The IIPC's existential inversion research groups currently help their members in a practical and substantial manner.

What is an *existential inversion research group?*

THE EXISTENTIAL INVERSION RESEARCH GROUP IS THE GROUP OF EXISTENTIAL INVERTERS WHOSE OBJECTIVE IS TO EXPERIENCE TEAM-PLANNED EXISTENTIAL INVERSION.

In terms of the technical, advanced, precocious planning of one's physical life, existential inversion is the most effective endeavor that a human consciousness can propose. Existential inversion undeniably super charges the individual's evolutionary performance maximally.

Existential inverters rely on constant full-time dedication in order to execute their life's program, usually before reaching the age of 26, which is generally accepted as the age of biological maturity.

In the process of existential inversion, the consciousness, while taking the first steps towards adulthood, acquires a new inner perspective or undergoes intraconsciential recycling.

What is *intraconsciential recycling?*

Intraconsciential recycling is a voluntary, self-induced internal recycling. It is the *greatest possible inner reform* that can be technically and rationally planned.

Existential inversion permits the *healthy* and *early start* of the executive phase of human life (typically spanning from 36 to 70 years of age) while one is still in the preparatory period – from 1 to 35 years of age.

At this point it is useful to ask the following question:

What healthy or sick consequences did your adolescence bring into your adult life?

The answer to this question indicates the level of your consciential maturity.

It is always worthwhile to take advantage of the current evolutionary moment in order to renew what we can. One hour today is worth three hours tomorrow.

The past should only exist in terms of the lessons it has left us. Aside from the educational aspects of the past, we should only interest ourselves in the present-future.

THE IMMUTABILITY OF OPINIONS INCREASES IN DIRECT PROPORTION TO PHYSICAL AGE, AS A FUNCTION OF NEOPHOBIA AND THE CRYSTALLIZATION OF ROUTINES.

8. HUMAN MATURITY

What is *human maturity?*

Human maturity is the inner state in which the development of the personality is complete.

Biologically speaking, maturity is reached after the age of 26 when the consolidation of the extremities or epiphyses of the human bones has taken place.

Human maturity expresses or should express a maximal recuperation of cons by the consciousness in this intraphysical life.

What is a *con?*

A CON IS A HYPOTHETICAL UNIT OF MEASUREMENT OF THE LUCIDITY LEVEL OF A CONSCIOUSNESS WHO HAS BEEN REBORN INTO MATTER ON THIS PLANET.

The full set of cons is lost by the consciousness during the funneling effect of rebirth into dense matter. Little by little, cons are partially recuperated during the development of human life.

The following are some examples of recuperation of *greater* cons: tachypsychic (extremely quick) rational thought; capacity for the logical association of ideas in the analysis of things in general; natural clairvoyant capacity.

All these attributes were freely enjoyed by the lucid consciousness through the emotional body (psychosoma) while in the extraphysical dimension, before using the current human instrument.

Human maturity comprises the final part of the executive phase of life that occurs in the span between 36 and 70 years of physical age (on average).

THE LEVEL OF RECUPERATION OF CONS SHOWS THE QUALITY OF THE HUMAN CONSCIOUSNESS' MOST RECENT INTERMISSIVE COURSE.

The most intelligent course of action for the human consciousness is to invest heavily (culture, intellectuality) in the attributes of the mental body (mentalsoma).

A major aspiration of every evolved human consciousness is to reach the condition of hyperacuity during the period of physical maturity.

What is *hyperacuity?*

Hyperacuity is the condition of maximum lucidity of the human consciousness achieved through a recuperation of all possible cons.

A condition contrary to hyperacuity is existential robotization.

What is *existential robotization?*

Existential robotization is the condition in which the human consciousness is still extremely tropospheric and excessively enslaved by intraphysical, animal life, *immersed* deep within the unthinking masses.

It is always hoped that by the time human maturity has been reached, the person will also have reached sexual maturity. As a result, the physically mature person will also have consolidated their social condition, by forming an evolutionary duo with another consciousness.

What is an *evolutionary duo?*

An evolutionary duo is the condition in which 2 consciousnesses interact positively in mutual evolution, that is, *cooperative evolution by two.*

There are *couples* who, despite the plenitude of sincere love that each partner devotes to the other, do not fulfill each other. This is why they decide to procreate or generate another human life.

This demonstrates, with indisputable logic, the influence of animal instincts over human consciousnesses.

There are *evolutionary duos* who, despite the plenitude of mutual affection and discernment that they enjoy from one another, do not fulfill each other, *not even* with the gestation of other human lives. They naturally aspire to much more.

From this is born the great maxifraternal works by two. It demonstrates, with irrefutable logic, a condition of advanced consciential maturity.

These two types of projects – one for having children and the other for evolving through interconsciential assistance – evidence the existence of two distinct levels of evolution of the consciousness: one being common and primary; the other being undeniably advanced.

Against facts there are no arguments, regardless of whom or where they come from.

Anticosmoethical competition must always be avoided in the actions of an evolutionary duo.

ONE FACTOR THAT MUST BE CONSIDERED IN THE CONSTITUTION OF AN EVOLUTIONARY DUO IS THE CONDITION OF THE INCOMPLETE COUPLE, WHEN PROBLEMATIC.

What is an *incomplete couple?*

An incomplete couple is a man and a woman who never actually constitute an intimate couple (a couple that engages in complete sexual acts), but maintain strong affective ties.

The maintenance of healthy incomplete couples depends on the social limits of friendship and the general interdependence of the non-promiscuous individuals.

It is worth pointing out that the human body requires special attention when mature.

After 45 years of age, every person's *organic machine* exhibits some natural deterioration, even if minimal.

During the phase of physical maturity, the consciousness should perform a self-analysis with respect to their weak and strong traits.

What is a *strong trait?*

A *strong trait* is a positive component or a virtue in the structure of one's consciential microuniverse that propels that consciousness' evolution.

Examples of strong traits: the great mathematician's capacity for concentration and elaboration of thought; the unique manual ability of the artisan.

It is intelligent to identify one's strongest personal trait, or megastrong trait in order to use it in the self-scrutinizing combat against weak traits in general, especially one's *megaweak trait.*

What is a *weak trait?*

A weak trait is a defect or psychological fissure in the structure of one's consciential micro-universe that the consciousness has not yet been able to overcome.

Examples of weak traits: the smoking habit of the lung specialist, highly qualified in the advanced treatment of human lungs; the talented but tardy artist, unable to correctly fulfill professional commitments.

The weak point is always an impediment to the acceleration of the consciousness' evolution.

*I*T IS ALWAYS INTELLIGENT TO IDENTIFY ONE'S WEAKEST PERSONAL TRAIT OR MEGAWEAK TRAIT *IN ORDER TO COMBAT IT USING ONE'S* MEGASTRONG TRAIT.

In general, every major mistake committed by the intraphysical consciousness is accompanied by its respective *in-*

ner repression. With time, the repressions accumulate and the person becomes narrow-minded.

During the phase of human maturity, a lucid individual needs to calculate his life's net balance in order to establish how much of his existential program he has already realized. There is nothing better, in this process of evaluation or renewal, than performing an existential recycling.

What is *existential recycling?*

Existential recycling is a technique wherein human consciousnesses change their existential perspective.

The consciousness reaches psychological or human maturity after the human body has reached biological maturity. However, the vast majority of people still lack holomaturity.

What is *holomaturity?*

Holomaturity is the personal condition of integrated maturity, that is: *first,* the biological or organic maturity of the soma; *second,* psychological or cerebral, social and human maturity; *third,* holosomatic maturity, relative to the conscientization (awareness) of the holosoma, retrocognitions, previous lives, and multidimensionality.

All this affects the level of personal lucidity with respect to one's holomemory.

What is *holomemory?*

Holomemory is a causal, compound, integral, multimillenary, multidimensional, uninterrupted, personal memory. It retains all facts related to the experiences of a particular consciousness. It is also called *multimemory* or *polymemory.*

WHEN APPLIED IN DAILY LIFE, HOLOMATURITY TAKES THE HUMAN CONSCIOUSNESS TO UNIMAGINABLE LEVELS OF SELF-AWARENESS.

In terrestrial life, we base and utilize our great stock of knowledge in the *genetic memory* of our brain. In extraphysical life, we establish and utilize our great stock of knowledge in our integral memory, our causal memory or holomemory.

The gap between the 2 memories determines the degree of our *consciential restriction* in the process of consecutive human lives.

What is *self-conscientiality?*

Self-conscientiality is the quality of the level of self-knowledge that is imperative for the consciousness.

The megaknowledge offered by self-conscientiality leads the individual to multidimensional self-conscientization (self-awareness).

What is *multidimensional self-conscientization?*

Multidimensional self-conscientization is the condition wherein a human consciousness has achieved mature lucidity with regards to consciential life in the evolved state of multidimensionality. This state is attained as a result of having conscious projections in non-physical dimensions.

The most intelligent intraphysical consciousnesses are the ones who are interested in human life as well as the extraphysical dimensions that are directly related to their current life and immediate future.

At this point, it is appropriate to pose a personal question:

On a scale of 1 to 5, what is your level of human maturity?

IN THE SAME WAY THAT WE HAVE SEVERAL TYPES OF MEMORY, INTELLIGENCE AND VEHICLES OF MANIFESTATION, WE ALSO HAVE SEVERAL EGOS TO BE DEVELOPED.

This means that in human life we can act as different, but authentic, centered characters or personalities.

Generally speaking, it becomes impractical to develop several of these egos at the same time, because one can predominate, monopolize and disastrously overrun the others.

Intraconsciential shocks are generally inevitable in cases where there is a multiplicity of personalities. That is why we always choose one ego to predominate, suppressing or eclipsing the others, even if temporarily.

For instance, *a promiscuous conquering ego* can not live in the same house, or more appropriately, *in the same soma* (human body) with *a philosophical ego.*

In this consciential era, mentalsomatic studies recommend that we *permanently* suppress the following egos, if possible: the *good life* ego, the *sexually immature* ego and the *mystical* ego, still enslaved by the *belly-brain.* Mentalsomatic studies also recommend that we develop the following egos: the *practical philosopher* ego and the *self-aware energizer* ego or the *interconsciential assistant* ego. The best is to choose a more evolved role or ego through which we can manifest ourselves on earth.

According to conscientiology, the following is a logical theory on the personality in evolution:

INDIVIDUALS CAN ONLY GAIN EVOLUTIONARILY WHEN THEY EVALUATE THEIR LEVEL OF CONSCIENTIZATION.

9. Existential Program

What is *existential completism?*

Existential completism is the comfortable condition of having satisfactorily completed one's *existential program.* This includes acts and works by the human consciousness that were previously planned during the most recent intermissive period.

Existential completism can only be attained through the able administration of the consciousness' *life projects.*

Human consciousnesses are existential completists if they have fulfilled the existential program within the allocated sector and level – irrespective of whether the existential program was a greater or lesser one.

Although interdependence is inevitable, it should not prevent us from doing what we must do in the execution of our existential program. Interdependence should in fact help.

There are *existential completists* who are totally unaware of their existential miniprograms. They live their existences and realize their work in a spontaneous, non-reflective and *para-instinctive* fashion without any conscious options.

The following are examples of common existential completists: the outstanding surgeon with decades of service rendered; the conventional writer, acclaimed as an intellectual, who has received all the laurels in his or her field.

THE EXISTENTIAL COMPLETIST'S REWARD IS TO CHOOSE A *BETTER SOMA* FOR THE NEXT MULTI-EXISTENTIAL EVOLUTIONARY PERIOD.

There are already human consciousnesses who are existential multicompletists.

What is an *existential multicompletist?*

An existential multicompletist is a consciousness who has satisfactorily executed more than one existential program.

This takes place, of course, using more than 1 human body and energetic body in more than 1 consecutive lifetime, epoch and intraphysical society, with an assistantial link occurring between the successive existential programs. This is called *existential multicompletism.*

There are consciousnesses who work for many centuries, in several human lifetimes, in the area of human education; others who work as religious professionals; and others still, who work in a specific sector of the arts, science or politics.

What is *existential incompletism?*

Existential incompletism is the uncomfortable, chronic and frustrating condition experienced by the human consciousness as a result of an incomplete, unsatisfactory execution of the existential program, which was previously planned during the most recent intermissive period.

Existential incompletism can result in a *premature desoma* or the early deactivation of the human body, before the time originally planned.

The greatest triumph of the human consciousness is existential completism.

However, the achievement of existential completism depends on the relationship of a consciousness with their evolutionary group and a personal code of principles to live by on earth.

A human consciousness without existential completism is like a bee without honey.

There are extreme cases of existential incompletism, some apparently without solution, such as the obese dietitian, the heart and lung specialist who smokes, or the demented psychiatrist.

Examples of ostensive and most common cases of existential incompletism are the businessman who becomes a drug dealer, the driver who becomes a traffic assassin, and the politician who drowns in *fraud.*

In the voluntary and satisfactory execution of the existential program, a consciousness has to clearly define their personal goals and tasks for each phase of existence, from cradle to grave.

IN SOME RARE CASES, A HELPER SUGGESTS OR INFORMS THE CONSCIOUSNESS WITH RESPECT TO SOME CLAUSE OF THE EXISTENTIAL PROGRAM.

This only happens in some *existential maxiprograms* that are more universalistic and involve the development of collective, maxifraternal interests and repercussions.

The most common scenario, in the case of the *existential miniprogram*, is for intention and personal effort to guide the already physically mature person to the gradual execution of his or her high priority tasks, without any traumatic changes or *evolutionary rape.*

When the person identifies the directives of their existential program in greater detail, it usually results in the discovery of essential gaps or omissions in the execution of certain parts of the existential program. At this point, the individual can receive an existential moratorium.

What is an *existential moratorium?*

An existential moratorium is an extension of human life given to deserving consciousnesses as a result of their efforts and fraternal accomplishments. This is done in order for them to correct omissions or endeavor to execute uncompleted tasks not yet accomplished in a reasonable fashion.

The existential moratorium is the positive postponing of the deactivation of the human body, or a *delayed desoma.*

There are two types of existential moratorium. The first is the lesser type, or *existential minimoratorium,* which is deficit based and peculiar to existential incompletism. The second is the greater type, or *existential maximoratorium,* a wholesale approach which is surplus based and characteristic of existential completism. The existential maximoratorium is a further healthier achievement with respect to the results of the life program.

THE EXISTENTIAL MORATORIUM IS THE RESULT OF THE DIRECT AND COSMOETHICAL INTERCESSION OF THE EVOLUTIONOLOGIST.

The time complement provided by an existential moratorium can vary from months to decades.

One may receive 2 or 3 existential moratoriums. They can include the *organic recycling* of the soma of the person receiving the moratorium. As well, there are extremely rare conditions of *existential moratoriums in group* (a group of people receiving a life extension).

After passing through the *bottleneck of subhumanity* and its remnant effects, the tendency of consciousnesses, in their continuous evolution, is to have discernment gradually predominate in their consciential micro-universe and to prioritize, centralize, and dedicate themselves full time to consciential gestations.

What is *consciential gestation?*

Consciential gestation is the evolutionary productivity of the human consciousness who is focused on the execution of *fraternal endeavors* and the implementation of renewing and libertarian ideas, within the framework of their existential program.

Consciential gestations can be aided by the intelligent use of conscientiometry.

What is *conscientiometry?*

Conscientiometry is the discipline that studies the measurement of the consciousness, through the resources and methods offered by conscientiology.

In many cases, consciential gestation involves making human gestation and its consequences – physical demands and time expenditures – a secondary priority.

THE EVOLUTIONARY DUO'S CONSCIENTIAL GESTATIONS CONSTITUTE A HEALTHY EXCEPTION-CONDUCT IN THE INTRAPHYSICAL DIMENSION.

The consciousness who has chosen consciential gestation chooses not to raise 1 to 3 children, for example, in order to work at the high priority task of assisting the evolution of thousands of people with whom they have no blood tie as well as extraphysical consciousnesses.

This posture represents leaving behind a primitive *animal life* in order to live fully in an advanced *consciential life*, in accordance with one's extraphysical hometown (extraphysical origin).

The *life plan* is analyzed under other multidimensional and multiexistential lenses, with its focus being the current and upcoming existences on earth. This is the task of the small but lucid element (*assistantial consciousness*) within a more extensive, all-inclusive and advanced structure (multidimensional *assistantial team*).

Choosing maxifraternity guides one to the intelligent search for consciential self-relay from that point on.

What is *consciential self-relay?*

Consciential self-relay or multiexistential continuism constitutes the greatest possible intertwining of the essential, evolutionary acts of one human life with those of the next, and other lives to come, in a continuous productive series (*seriality*) of completed existential programs.

Consciential gestations, with consecutive multiexistential self-relays involving human multidimensional tasks performed in a team effort, can demand the use of a macrosoma.

What is a *macrosoma?*

A MACROSOMA IS A SUPER CUSTOMIZED HUMAN BODY USED FOR THE EXECUTION OF A SPECIFIC EXISTENTIAL PROGRAM.

Personal organization that covers all sectors of human life and is also based on cosmoethics, is inevitably discovered and brought to the fore of daily concerns as result of consciential self-relay.

What is *cosmoethics?*

Cosmoethics – cosmic morality – is the foundation for all intersciential assistantial tasks and is the moral philosophy of conscientiology.

It is a set of principles that will lead one to make fewer mistakes. As such, cosmoethics eliminates the useless suffering of the human consciousness.

All *amorality* increases the percentage of personal errors.

A *"light"* cosmoethics does not resolve the human consciousness' evolutionary issues.

Our acts are either correct or incorrect in light of cosmoethics.

EACH HUMAN CONSCIOUSNESS HAS THEIR PERSONAL CODE OF COSMOETHICS THAT REFLECTS THE CODE OF THE COSMOS WITHIN THEM.

Do you feel cosmoethically responsible for your acts?

Cosmoethics is the reflection and experience of the multi-dimensional cosmic moral. It represents the essence of integral maturity and extends beyond the social moral or ethics appearing within any human classification.

The individual's attributes *(strong traits)* and flaws *(weak traits)* are seen from a different perspective. There is an increased possibility of improving the inner reform of the consciousness' micro-universe.

The individual considers his ego in relation to the simpler bad habits and addictions such as smoking, the definitive discarding of light and heavy drugs, and the elimination of the ordinary law of least effort.

In this way, men and women identify groupkarmic interprison and intraphysical melancholy.

What is *groupkarmic interprison?*

Groupkarmic interprison is the condition of an inextricability of consciousnesses within an evolutionary group, who have committed anticosmoethical acts in group. They remain imprisoned with or tied to their marginal evolutionary companions until they are able to cosmoethically *rearrange* their path.

Anticosmoethical groupkarmic interprison is caused jointly among accomplices of antisocial machines; extermination groups; Mafias; inquisitions; human torture; war; terrorist acts; and genocide.

Groupkarmic interprison provokes intraphysical melancholy in the human consciousness.

What is *intraphysical melancholy?*

Intraphysical melancholy is a condition of profound frustration experienced by a person prior to the deactivation of their human body. It is generated by the dissatisfaction with oneself for having neglected and ultimately failed to achieve some consciential endeavor in the field of assistantial universalism, which the person was invited to undertake.

Intraphysical melancholy appears during human maturity or the executive phase of one's physical life. It can be accompanied by longing, nostalgia and sadness, which are qualities peculiar to the *foreigner syndrome.*

THE FIRST SYMPTOM OF INTRAPHYSICAL MELANCHOLY IS A PERSISTENT SADNESS THAT CAN LEAD TO APATHY OR ABULIA.

In certain cases, intraphysical melancholy can attract multicentenary intruders and, as a result, provoke a state of profound depression.

Intraphysical melancholy can lead a person to suffer from permanent crises of depression and a lack of self-esteem that require prolonged therapeutic attention. Conscientiotherapy is usually recommended in these cases.

The acquisition of a new perspective or the rational recycling of human life definitively cures intraphysical melancholy.

What is *universalism?*

Universalism is the set of ideas derived from the universality of the basic laws of nature and the cosmos. As a result of the consciousness' natural evolution, universalism inevitably becomes their prevailing cosmic philosophy, being the most intelligent and useful one with respect to the dynamics of evolution.

Applied universalism is synonymous with anti-egoism, cosmism, cosmopolitanism, *disarmamentism*, eclecticism, ecumenism, generalism, *intergalacticism*, internationalism, maxifraternity, *multiculturalism*, multidimensionality, multidisciplinarity, *globalization*, polykarmality, polyglotism, *supranationalism*.

The experience of *social* universalism is the first step towards the experience of *multidimensional* universalism. It tends to standardize cultural principles and norms everywhere.

Through universalism, the person in frank development arrives at the personal classification of their tasks, interests, and objectives, within the consolation task, the clarification task and penta.

What is *the consolation task?*

The consolation task is an elementary, personal or groupal assistantial task. It is easier to execute, more pleasant within the human social environment and brings immediate gratification as a payoff for the efforts of the practitioner. It deals with the maximum consolation of tropospheric intraphysical consciousnesses, or rather, those who are needy, socially impaired and inexperienced in regards to evolution.

Is the consolation task a *palliative?*

Yes, the consolation task is a palliative. It is a simpler task that *pleases* needy people by employing emotions and euphemisms. It provides immediate results for the practitioners who frequently proselytize, emphasize mysticism, appeal to religious or political demagogy and moralist conventions.

The consolation task is always superficial. It never encourages the complete renovation of those who are helped. The existential recycling that it offers is invariably shallow.

At its core, the consolation task is still a *light brainwashing*, based on the *psychological crutches* of outdated formulas, maintaining dependency and repression.

THE CONSOLATION TASK IS NOT AN IDEAL ASSISTANTIAL TASK. FOR MANY PEOPLE, IT CONSTITUTES COMPLACENCY OR DEVIATION FROM THE EXISTENTIAL PROGRAM.

This complacency or deviation refers to the execution of an advanced existential program that was planned during the intermissive course.

What is the *clarification task?*

The clarification task is a more advanced, personal or groupal assistantial task. It always appears once the consolation task has already been experienced. It is more difficult to execute and is generally antipathetic within the human social environment. It provides only long term gratification, which is realized during the intermissive period, after the deactivation of the human body.

The advanced clarification task deals with leading-edge relative truths that address individuals, groups, institutions, societies, multidimensional objects and realities in general.

The clarification task is undeniably different from the consolation task.

The clarification task is surgical in nature. It promotes profound recycling and, in fact, intimately modifies the intraphysical consciousness in a visceral, practical and objective manner.

The clarification task offers more definitive assistantial solutions. It evolves against the flow of ordinary human concerns. It exalts self-scrutiny and personal discernment. It dispenses with personality cults. It leads people to think for themselves in order to liberate them from millenary oppression by instincts, unhealthy dependence and sanctification.

From among the best, super-endowed individuals of the new human generations who are conscious of existential completism, conscientiologists currently seek those who intend to dedicate themselves to *cosmoethical clarification tasks* along multidimensional lines.

Within this context, researchers give preference to couples, including youths, who currently comprise *evolutionary duos* having a high level of lucidity.

THE CLARIFICATION TASK FREES THE CONSCIOUSNESS FROM THE CYCLE OF SUCCESSIVE, REPETITIVE LIVES. FOR THIS REASON, IT IS THE UNIT BY WHICH SELF-EVOLUTION CAN BE MEASURED.

The level of our evolutionary competence with respect to our undertakings is anatomized by the net-balance of our existential completism or incompletism, our existential moratorium or multicompletism, our human gestations or consciential endeavors, our consolation or clarification task, and of our consciential self-relay.

What is *penta?*

Penta is the *p*ersonal *en*ergetic *ta*sk. It is a multidimensional task that consists of daily energetic assistance rendered to others for the remainder of the practitioner's life. The penta practitioner receives constant assistance from helpers. In general, it arises after the individual has experienced the clarification task.

Penta is an effective technique for maintaining human beings connected with their consciential, evolutionary and extraphysical origin, that exists beyond the terrestrial troposphere. This connection is maintained without any antiquated and undesirable subjugation to dogmatic *brainwashing* or *brain-shrinking* doctrines of any type.

Penta has extraphysical or multidimensional assistantial roots based on the helper of the practitioner and on the helper of those receiving assistance.

The gradual or joint execution of these three assistantial tasks – consolation, clarification and penta – leads the consciousness to consider as realistic the goal of becoming permanently-totally-intrusion-free.

What is *permanently-totally-intrusion-free?*

Permanently-totally-intrusion-free is the consciential quality and human condition of an individual who no longer suffers any type of intrusion.

The person who is permanently-totally-intrusion-free does not suffer from the frequent occurrence of unconscious intrusions that have affected all of humanity throughout the millennia, in successive lives and in the most varied of human societies. This person then becomes *conscious assistantial bait.*

IN THE CONDITION OF BEING PERMANENTLY-TOTALLY-INTRUSION-FREE, THE CONSCIOUSNESS EXECUTES MANY ASSISTANTIAL TASKS AS A CONSCIENTIAL EPICENTER.

What is a *consciential epicenter?*

A consciential epicenter is a person who becomes a pole of lucidity, assistantial reasoning, and is a fulcrum of operant multidimensional constructivism.

The flexibility of the energetic body is fundamental in the development of the consciential epicenter.

The consciential epicenter always has a well-consolidated physical base for the human body. This physical base is the material seat of their interdimensional assistantial work. This is the case even when the person travels frequently.

There are 4 basic types of consciential epicenter: the average but lucid human consciousness, the permanently-totally-intrusion-free individual, the Evolutionologist and the *Homo sapiens serenissimus.*

The consciential epicenter has a direct experiential relationship with advanced penta and the extraphysical assistantial facility.

What is an *extraphysical assistantial facility?*

The extraphysical assistantial facility is where intraphysical consciential epicenters perform their assistantial works of greater magnitude and where *parasanitary isolation* is established for the purpose of assisting sick extraphysical leaders and other cases of equal measure.

The numerous requests made of the penta practitioner by those in pursuit of the assistance provided through the extraphysical assistantial facility, through letters and other types of communication, evidence the level of the public's need for intersciential assistance everywhere.

As we can logically conclude, one can arrive at 60 years of age and be positive, lucid and beneficent, with healthy intentions and, more importantly, working in favor of others.

On the other hand, at the same age, one can be suffering from the initial stages of senility (senile psychosis), have bad habits, complain constantly, be pessimistic and grouchy, and be unproductive with regards to working in favor of others.

From this arise two pertinent questions:

DO YOU, AS A HUMAN BEING, FEEL MORE OR LESS ADAPTED TO THE ACTIVE EXECUTION OF YOUR EXISTENTIAL PROGRAM?

*Can you logically conceive, imagine or understand a **body** of philosophical, political or scientific **ideas,** having a rational and coherent beginning, middle and end, and providing the basic coordinates of your **life's plan,** that is better than this one?*

All of this is the summary of our personal and groupal experiences resulting from half a century of research, hypothesis and theories, many of which have already been published.

If you are able to logically and detachedly explain the broad practical reasons for our life with better concepts than those presented here, please communicate your discovery to this author, who will be forever grateful.

It is very difficult for a person to think extensively about the basic directives of evolutionary life, due to the influences of transitory human involvements.

From this arise the endless foolishness and superfluous immaturity in the ephemeral existence of all social beings.

These foolish and immature tendencies number in the millions, ranging from the most simple and insignificant to the most sophisticated lucubrations of human beings.

Examples of these types are abundant everywhere and block the free development of the consciousness.

ONE OF THE MOST FOOLISH OF HUMAN ENDEAVORS IS THE COLLECTION OF ARMS. THIS ONLY WORSENS THE COLLECTOR'S ENERGETIC ENVIRONMENT.

10. PREPARATION FOR THE NEXT LIFE

What is most intelligent for the *well-being of the human individual?*

The most intelligent for the well-being and comfort of the human individual is to begin the preparation of the next intraphysical life, here and now, while more or less healthy, lucid and active in the body of flesh.

What do we wish for our next life? Greater discernment? Maturity at an earlier age? An advanced task of clarification? Completion of our existential program at a high level?

OUR CONCERNS REGARDING THE FUTURE ARE LEGITIMATE. OUR EVOLUTIONARY ASPIRATIONS ARE HEALTHY AND NATURAL.

For this, however, we need to think of our current possibilities within the law of action and reaction, or holokarma.

What is *holokarma?*

Holokarma is the union of three types of consciential actions and reactions – egokarma, groupkarma and polykarma – within the principles of cause and effect operating in the evolutionary structure of the consciousness.

Holokarma has a decisive influence on the multiexistential cycle, the programming of human life, the selection of elements of the evolutionary group, and on the fundamental directives of the consciousness' destiny, through the wise mediation of the Evolutionologist.

Discernment allows you to untangle the twists and turns of your holokarmic account, its causes and effects, actions and reactions regarding the cosmos, in your personal and group evolution.

This possibility suggests to your more alert consciousness the fundamental and calculable directives that can be established for your next human rebirth on this planet, while you are still here in dense physical life.

This is the first condition required for the discernment and evaluation of consciential self-relay.

AFTER MANY MILLENNIUMS, WE ARRIVED AT THIS POINT AS MERE PASSIVE SPECTATORS OF OUR PERSONAL HISTORY.

Up until yesterday, we lived without any awareness of our objectives.

We made decisions without thinking about the quality of our consciential destiny. We allowed ourselves to be dragged along between various dimensions, times, cultures, human and extraphysical societies, like blind persons, anonymously immersed in our evolutionary group.

Maturity, however, challenges us.

Each one of us needs, here and now, to put a *stop* to this precarious condition of enslaving and subhuman unconsciousness.

It is important that we begin to participate as *self-aware protagonists* with explicit determination and lucid choice in the detailed formulation of our immediate future.

It is essential that we include in this equation as much self-scrutiny as possible, with our greatest *intelligence* and a maximum of bioenergetic performance.

What is *intelligence?*

Intelligence is the capacity for learning, comprehending and easily adapting to renovations. It includes perception, comprehension and intellect (intellectuality), when an individual demonstrates acumen, sharpness or perspicacity regarding the cosmos, consciousnesses, energies, ideas and objects.

Intelligence is the most valuable and sought after commodity on the planet today. It constitutes the sum total of the capacities of learning, logic, memorization, adaptation to an environment or dimension, beyond personal motivation and effort.

We all have various intelligences, for example: contextual, corporal, spatial, experimental, internal, linguistic, logical and musical.

AMONG OUR MULTIPLE MODULES OF INTELLIGENCE, THREE CAN BE EMPHASIZED: CULTURAL, PARAPSYCHIC AND COMMUNICATIVE.

Our modules of intelligence allow us to choose which body – the human body, the emotional body or the *mentalsoma* – to prioritize in the development of our priority actions.

What is the *mentalsoma?*

The mentalsoma is the mental body or the parabody of discernment of the consciousness. It is your most sophisticated vehicle of manifestation.

The parabody of discernment allows one to list the minimal, practical and useful factors to be considered in consciential research. Self-research is the most important of all.

For example:

The act of accurately observing phenomena until a provisional conclusion about them is reached.

The acceptance of probable determinism.

The central topic chosen to be researched.

The definition of the thesis in question.

The practical application of the defended thesis.

The phenomena detected in intraphysical and extraphysical life.

The arguments and ideas isolated in favor of the original thesis.

The relationships between similar ideas.

The practical occurrences that corroborate theoretical expositions.

The relative leading-edge truth obtained with respect to the original thesis addressed.

The mentalsoma exalts the value of analysis, the association of ideas, relative certainty, comparison, comprehension, knowledge, cosmoethics, exactness, holomemory, imagination, investigation, critical judgment, logic, parapsychism, reason, wisdom and initial synthesis.

In the study of the mentalsoma – *mentalsomatics* – the incontestable reality of the thosene clearly stands out.

What is a *thosene?*

According to conscientiology, the thosene is the unit of manifestation (act, action, gesture, posture) of the consciousness, considering *tho*ught or idea (conception), *sen*timent or emotion and consciential *en*ergy to be inextricably connected.

Thosenes with an accentuated *sen* (sentiment, emotion and desire) are the least trustworthy and have a greater degree of pathology.

The *phytothosene* is the rudimentary thosene of plants.

The *graphothosene* is the thosenic signature or the peculiar style of the author in all modalities of art, endeavors and personal undertakings.

The *hyperthosene* is the original idea of the inventor or discoverer.

The *megathosene* is the correct, cosmoethical thought.

The *monothosene* is the fixed idea of the mentally ill.

The *retrothosene* is the innate idea with which we all are born.

The *sexthosene* is the sexual fantasy, almost always only thought about.

The *xenothosene* is the invasive mental wedge from another consciousness.

The *sense of discernment* indicates that human conflicts can occur between: right and wrong – *correction*; the constantly renewed relative truth and the unverifiable absolute truth – *rationality*; truth and lies – *self-corruption*; knowledge and ignorance – *holomaturity*; the best and the worst – *prioritization*; direct personal experience and spontaneous faith – *evolutionality*; good and evil – *Manicheanism*; current consensus and the consensus outdated by facts – *actuality*; the ideal and the ordinary – *maquillage*.

The search for self-knowledge makes one emphasize the irrefutable superiority of the mentalsoma's evolved attributes over those of the other vehicles of manifestation.

Have you discovered the importance of the mentalsoma?

IT IS ALWAYS WORTH THE EFFORT REQUIRED TO UTILIZE THE IDLE CAPACITY OF OUR MENTALSOMA THROUGH RATIONALITY.

What is *rationality?*

RATIONALITY IS THE ACT OR EFFECT OF REASONING, WITH THE MORE-OR-LESS LOGICAL INTERCONNECTION OF JUDGMENTS OR THOUGHTS.

Reasoning is the same as *reason.*

Only rational self-scrutiny offers the human consciousness self-evaluation, whether as one who is secure and self-sufficient, or one who is in lack, dependent and irresolute – the common *butterfly seeker.*

On a scale of 1 to 5, how much do you value consciential maturity?

Do you effectively apply rationality in your everyday life?

Rationality allows one to discover the importance of holomaturity and, consequently, universalism, the broad vision of the harmony of life principles.

How do you experience universalism?

All these occurrences engender an elevated sense of community in a person.

What is a *sense of community?*

A sense of community is personal judgment and experiential understanding relative to the community, considered to be a fundamental structure of human society.

We are all reborn with dual citizenship: intraphysical and extraphysical. Extraphysical citizenship predominates in consciential evolution.

Does your sense of community need improvement?

Human consciousnesses need to live with their feet on the ground and their mentalsoma in the cosmos. This evolved attitude leads the interested individual to cogitate about multidimensionality.

> *What is multidimensionality?*

Multidimensionality is the notion and consequent experience of the lucid consciousness not only in the physical dimension but also in other consciential dimensions.

Multidimensional life is indispensable for all of us.

OUR CONSCIOUSNESS DOES NOT ACTUALLY INSERT ITSELF INTO MATTER. ONLY OUR ENERGIES ARE ROOTED IN THE HUMAN BODY.

> *How do you experience your multidimensionality in a more dynamic way?*

Stemming from the personal awareness of multidimensionality, consciousnesses desire to take advantage of their energies, time, space and opportunities. Thus arise preoccupations with fraternal assistance to all.

Conventional sciences – *dermatologies of the consciousness* (superficial approaches) – with their physicalist Newtonian-Cartesian paradigm, despite their impressive accomplishments over the last 4 centuries, have failed abundantly in their attempts to clarify the nature of the ego.

This is because they have not included multidimensional and cosmoethical reality in their fundamental theories. Nor have they discovered the *multidimensional reality* that intrinsically and indissolubly exists in the *social* and *psychological reality* of the human being *(mind-matter dilemma)*, both individually and in group.

Fraternal assistance can be the superficial, amateurish pleasant improvement of the gastric mucosae of others, in other words, temporary consolation. Or it can be the more difficult assistance required for permanent personal renovation regarding the ideas and neural connections of those assisted, in other words, true clarification.

Sooner or later, discernment leads one to choose the clarification task over the consolation task.

Do you already practice the *clarification task?*

The following are 3 practical examples of the clarification task: write a book that is not just literary or mercantilist, but clarifying or informational for the readers; give a class on advanced topics in conscientiality; strengthen an ill person, not only by consoling them, but by actually clarifying them, in such a way that they think about the development and consequences of their illness.

UPON PERFORMING THE CLARIFICATION TASK, WE NEED TO IMPROVE THE APPLICATION OF OUR CONSCIENTIAL ENERGIES AND PARAPSYCHISM.

This action inevitably ends up leading the consciousness to a more evolved parapsychism.

What is *parapsychism?*

Parapsychism is the set of the human consciousness' advanced perceptions, beyond the 5 basic senses of the human body, utilizing energies, animism, and advanced interconsciential exchanges.

Are you working on your parapsychic reeducation?

The beginning of parapsychic reeducation is based on the control of consciential energies, which leads one to an energetic springtime.

What is *energetic springtime?*

Energetic springtime is the personal, more or less long lasting condition wherein one's consciential energies exhibit a peak level of health and constructiveness. When brief, it is an energetic minispringtime, when prolonged it is an energetic maxispringtime.

THE AFFECTIVE-SEXUAL CONDITION OF A HONEYMOON CAN BE A PERIOD OF AN EVOLUTIONARY DUO'S ENERGETIC MINI OR MAXISPRINGTIME.

Do you apply your consciential energies having in mind your *evolutionary file?*

The basic goal of parapsychism is the indispensable bioenergetic self-balancing or a deliberate relative self-cure. This facilitates the development of individual abnegated assistance to others according to the laws of cosmoethics.

At what level is your daily experience of the cosmoethic?

Following are three examples of practical cosmoethical experiences: to put aside your personal egoism when making a decision that affects the rights of other consciousnesses; to be sincere and loyal in your dealings with others; to eliminate self-corruption in relation to your coworkers.

Do you think it is important to establish the foundation of your next human life through the application of this series of advanced consciential acts?

Cosmoethics recommends that you prioritize your work according to the following principle: it is always best to exert the majority of your effort in favor of others, even if it requires personal sacrifice, rather than in your own favor, without any personal sacrifice, in the interest of dynamizing Conscious Evolution.

Cosmoethics involves personal incorruptibility, which eliminates all corrupting thoughts. Although small and apparently innocuous, corrupting thoughts, when considered rationally, are pathological and block personal progress.

Just as mental peccadillos exist (*pathothosenes*), peccadillos also exist in dreams (*oneirothosenes*).

Our holomemory registers the reality that we create – ideas, emotions and energies, even when very subtle – all the time, wherever we are, without any gaps or mistakes.

As you can see, we count on the following effective resources, as well as many others, in the preparation for our next life: balance the relationships with the elements of our human families; employ cosmoethics in all of our major decisions; achieve a mastery of the preventive vibrational state as a daily practice; apply oneself in the production of projections with continuous consciousness; ensure that the clarification task predominates over the consolation task in our acts; be a part of an evolutionary duo specialized in consciential gestations; and predispose oneself to the execution of penta for the rest of one's human life.

11. DEACTIVATION OF THE HUMAN BODY

What is the *final projection?*

The final projection is the intraphysical consciousness' irreversible, definitive, unique and absolute out-of-body experience. In the final projection, the consciousness of the conscious human projector leaves the physical body, goes to an extraphysical community and stays there. It is a projection of the consciousness with no return.

This final projection is the same as desoma (deactivation of the soma), first death or biological death. It is the inevitable disconnection of the consciousness from the soma.

PROJECTIONS IN WHICH THE CONSCIOUSNESS REMAINS LUCID COMBAT AND ELIMINATE MANY FEARS, INCLUDING THANATOPHOBIA.

What is *thanatophobia?*

Thanatophobia is the unhealthy fear that a person experiences regarding the inevitable and expected death of the human body.

Conscious projections eliminate this and many other phobias, as well as many minor illnesses and unpleasant inner conditions during terrestrial life.

Conscious projections annul the negative effects that physical death or desoma otherwise has on one's daily life.

Upon leaving the human body, the lucid consciousness manifests itself through a *body other* than the soma. In most cases, this body is the psychosoma or emotional body, which is lighter and subtler than the physical body.

In addition, the consciousness experiences life in a *dimension different* from the human atmosphere, a *paratropospheric* dimension, which corresponds extraphysically to the layer extending from sea level up to an altitude of 6.25 miles (10 kilometers).

These occurrences always obey a fixed pattern all over the world, differing only in the interpretations given to them by the projectors themselves. These interpretations vary according to the projectors' cultural and social principles, as well as the conditioning and repression that their upbringing and education imposed on them.

Those who are more universalistic and less sectarian better interpret and receive more value from conscious experiences outside the human body.

They more easily discover their status as consciousnesses in evolution within a period of human, animal existence. And they more quickly and easily recover the facts regarding the reality of their extraphysical hometown, the place where they resided before being reborn.

HUMAN LIFE HAS NEVER, IN ANY CIVILIZATION, REACHED AS ADVANCED A LEVEL OF EVOLUTION AS IT HAS TODAY.

Ordinary people have currently a less superficial concept regarding the *broad range* of their potentialities.

The protection of human rights is generally clearer and more greatly supported by the governments of the most influential nations.

Citizens' health is currently better defended. Because of this, they can live longer, have more time for leisure and are motivated to work, study, and experience what they wish.

The visible effects of an improved human life are occurring all over the Earth. Among these, the natural increase in the elderly population (veterans of life) can be highlighted.

This fact has been generating problems for governments and raising questions within societies regarding productive leisure, social welfare, retirement and assistance to the elderly, as well as a reasonable and fruitful social life in their golden age.

What is the *golden age?*

A person who is 65 years or older is said to be a golden ager.

Among the assistance available to those of advanced age the work of specialists in thanatology is worth highlighting.

What is thanatology?

Thanatology is the science that studies the physical contexts of death, as well as related social, psychological, and medical-legal contexts.

Thanatologists work primarily in intensive care units assisting terminally ill patients, intraphysical consciousnesses who are on the verge of returning to their extraphysical state.

There are hospitals that specialize in gerontology, assisting geriatric patients or elderly men and women.

THE DEATH OF THE HUMAN BODY REPRESENTS A BRIEF OR EXTENDED POSTOPERATIVE PERIOD FOR THE CONSCIOUSNESSES ON EARTH.

The act of putting the human body out of commission, however, does not imply the final sleep, disappearance, eternal rest or the end of life for the consciousness who has spent the last six, seven or more decades vitalizing it.

The passage of death, or desoma, is the last thing that the human consciousness can *do well* while continuing to breathe in an animal body within this planetary atmosphere.

However, among the biggest follies, accompanied by great pomp and ceremony in the classic treatises of universal wisdom, are those dealing with the death of men and women.

The inner conflicts of the consciousness or those of intraconsciential origin do not simply disappear with the deactivation of the human body.

After the biological shock of the desoma, consciousnesses intimately continue being whatever they always were. The intimate structure of the consciential micro-universe continues to exist in exactly the same manner.

The most comfortable desoma is that of the existential completist, that personality who has completed all *clauses of their contract* of human experiences that were established before being reborn on earth.

The least comfortable desoma is, obviously, that of the person who commits suicide.

METAPHORICALLY SPEAKING, SENILITY IS A MUSICAL PIECE THAT TERMINATES LONG AFTER THE END.

One of the biggest losses felt by consciousnesses, aside from the loss of the physical body, is the lack of animal, sexual, sexchakral, or affective energy. This is one of the most common causes of postsomatic parapsychosis.

What is *postsomatic parapsychosis?*

Postsomatic parapsychosis is the condition in which consciousnesses have already lost their human body, but think, feel and conclude that they continue to exist *inside of it* and with it.

The body of emotions (psychosoma) is a perfect copy of the human body (soma), or more appropriately, the soma is a copy of the psychosoma. The psychosoma is much subtler and lighter than the soma. But, after cerebral death, a consciousness' awareness is usually clouded.

One no longer has lungs, but seems to continue breathing.

The personality no longer has a stomach, but feels hunger.

The consciousness no longer has sexual organs, but feels sexual excitability.

Thus, one exhibits reduced critical judgment in his or her manifestations in an environment that is very new relative to the habits of an entire lifetime lasting many decades.

Senile psychosis, arteriosclerosis, or even the very prevalent Alzheimer's disease can, in certain cases, represent a long, final human period that can diminish the extraphysical period of postsomatic parapsychosis.

This occurs with a multitude of elderly people.

The grumpy, grouchy old man, for example, without being aware of the consequences, constantly evokes or calls for certain companions, relatives or friends, often even from his childhood, who are already deceased, complaining about things and situations from the past which they experienced or were involved in together.

LEGIONS OF EVOKED CONSCIOUSNESSES, OUTSIDE OF THE HUMAN BODY, LIVE IN EXTRAPHYSICAL CONDITIONS OF INTENSE INNER LACK.

Such unhealthy *evocations,* bearing persistent sorrow and resentment, occur habitually through narration of cases that is repeated day after day by the elderly person, almost always with evident ironic insinuations, sarcasm or even hostility towards the deceased protagonist of their shared experiences.

This condition obviously provokes, chronic pathological and unhealthy *interconsciential intrusions* between the evoking intraphysical consciousness, in this case the persecutor, and the evoked extraphysical consciousness, the persecuted victim, who is recalled with repeated disaffection or persistent lamentations.

In countless occurrences of this type, the evoked consciousnesses are not fully aware of what is happening between them and the human evoker.

The evoked consciousnesses simply responds to the summons because likes attract. They become even more confused in their state of inner disturbance and are obviously incapable of exteriorizing balanced energies or comfortable sentiments to those they come in contact with. This is the case even though the evoked consciousnesses is coming from another consciential dimension.

These constant flows of *pathological thosenes* hit the evoking person straigtht on as an instantaneous disturbed response. This creates a vicious pathological cycle. Unfortunately, millions of persons live exactly like this.

The two stubborn consciousnesses can remain stuck or imprisoned with each other for five years, a decade or even longer.

This is why people can be classified as being *singular*, or isolated consciential units, or *plural*, when conscientially, mutually, pathologically, and constantly, stuck to each other.

It can happen that, once freed from each other, the person who was addicted to the evocations goes through desoma soon thereafter.

FOR THE MAJORITY OF PEOPLE, THE FULL EXECUTION PHASE OF THE EXISTENTIAL PROGRAM PRECEDES DEACTIVATION OF THE HUMAN BODY.

Intraphysical consciousnesses reach the golden age, as either completists or incompletists, with or without an existential moratorium, being *affable individuals* or difficult, grumpy, unhappy, pessimistic and hard to deal with. This indicates that they are experiencing a profound intraphysical melancholy, or that they are happy, optimistic and animated as a result of their intraphysical euphoria.

Intraphysical melancholy, as previously explained, is a condition of habitual sadness that the sullen mature person feels at the end of their human life as a result of being disillusioned by their own experiences, or rather, disappointed and unhappy in relation to their existential program.

What is *intraphysical euphoria?*

Intraphysical euphoria is the opposite of intraphysical melancholy. It is the habitual communicative happiness that the mature person feels, at the end of their human life, when they are satisfied for having reasonably accomplished their existential program. This is the condition that most predisposes one to having a positive, enhancing existential maxi-moratorium.

In regards to intraphysical melancholy and euphoria, the following is a very opportune question for the reader:

Are you a good fellow or an ill-tempered person?

As a golden ager, one should be used to facing the subjects previously addressed because, in this period, we are all closer to changing over to a different consciential dimension. And, logically, we must be prepared for this renovation, without fear or repression and free from the human foolishness surrounding these unpleasant themes, which are virtual taboos for the majority of people in certain societies, but an inevitable theme for us all.

There are people who erroneously *satisfy themselves with very little.* Very often, they are performing at sublevel (underachievement) with respect to their existential program. They may be lazy, applying the law of least effort, *procrastinating* and living in complacent apathy with respect to interpersonal assistance.

RETIREMENT IS NOT DEATH. IT CAN BE AN EXTREMELY FERTILE AND PRODUCTIVE PERIOD FOR THOSE WHO ARE STILL LUCID.

The *menopausal* period is not death for a woman. It can be the beginning of a useful phase of consciential gestation for the motivated intraphysical consciousness.

12. Return to Our Extraphysical Hometown

Inside each one of us, human personalities, we know that we will someday return to where we came from, a place outside of the terrestrial atmosphere.

There are those who have an acute sense of this reality since adolescence.

Others already know what they want to do in their new life since their early childhood.

OUR PERSONAL ORIGIN, A SUBTLE NON-PHYSICAL COMMUNITY, HAS VERY CHARACTERISTIC PROPERTIES THAT DIFFER FROM THE TERRESTRIAL ENVIRONMENT.

There we communicate through a subtler and lighter body. We are liberated from gravity.

We do not need to breathe. We dispense with food and drink.

In this other body, which is much older than the human body, we free ourselves from the subjugation of sex through our will and intention. We can not forget that the consciousness has no gender. What does have gender is the *sexsoma* or human body. However, this does not mean that we do not suffer the needs of all the human habits that we acquire. This is the case, as previously explained, in instances of postsomatic parapsychosis.

From this arise the problems of millions of extraphysical consciousnesses.

Accustomed to the human body and the immediate satisfaction of its demands, instincts and material appetites, day after day, over decades, consciousnesses – just like you and me – leave the body in the cemetery, but fail to leave behind the deeply rooted, carnal, human habits that the physical body created for them.

They do not perceive this greater reality. Sometimes they do not even want to consider this reality as a hypothesis for analysis.

They still feel like human beings and, irrationally, want to continue being human. This irrational intransigence then creates many extraphysical pathologies.

Postsomatic parapsychotics unconsciously crave the biochemical energy of the body that they lost. This means that they continue having appetite, thirst, human anxiety, exacerbated sexual desire, various needs and the continued desire to enjoy a human physical life equal to that of any one of us who continues here in physical life.

Obviously, this is now definitively impossible for them. This scenario of extraphysical reality is a truly lamentable irony.

The extraphysical environment and the new vehicle are much better, more malleable, functional and comfortable than the imprisoned, restricted life experienced while inside the human vehicle of flesh. The soma is a *XT,* the psychosoma is a *Pentium III*.

The extraphysical state is much less physical than the somatic state.

However, the ex-master of the house goes on living in his home as if nothing out of the ordinary had happened.

If one of us, while projected, enters his ex-house at night, in order to assist one of the children who reside there, he tries to chase us out, mistaking us for an invader of his property and an intruder of the personal domain of his home.

The ex-owner of the bakery tries to take care of his ex-clientele. He often becomes desperate because he is unable to converse with an ex-client. He approaches her, tries to communicate with her and even follows her home.

LEGIONS OF CONSCIOUSNESSES SUFFER THE EFFECTS OF THE ANTAGONISTIC, UNHEALTHY, BLIND AND CHAOTIC ENERGIES THAT THEY CONTINUALLY EXTERIORIZE.

The miser, now in another dimension, seeks to uselessly prevent his money from being divided among his family, extraphysically cursing at a fragile and needy relative. The relative may attend an umbanda ritual (Umbanda – syncretic doctrine with Afro-Brazilian fundaments) with the intention of relieving her disturbances, whereupon she is informed that she has an *extraphysical intruder* with her. Unreconciled, she goes to a spiritist center (Spiritism – Kardecism, neo spiritualism) and the mentor of the house tells her that she is suffering from *intrusion.*

All this gives rise to the intricate and complex problems of interconsciential intrusion for millions of extraphysical consciousnesses and human personalities who are unaware of interdimensionality and the interchange between consciential *macro*-worlds and *micro*-universes.

Conventional science *could not care less* about this raw and sad reality.

In this way, we suffer the unhealthy intrusion and influence of those with whom we had great affinity – often those personalities most cherished and remembered – because they are still dear to us. The purest, well-intentioned and most unforgettable affections can be transformed into *venomous energies.*

This entourage of sick extraphysical consciousnesses may be composed of our relatives, closest friends, most respected colleagues and acquaintances of an entire lifetime.

Extraphysical consciousnesses having a greater lucidity and interest recognize these regretful occurrences, want to help and truly do the best that they can. They are, however, not able to meet the assistantial needs of this situation.

Each one of us has an unshakable and inalienable intentionality.

AFTER ATTAINING A CERTAIN LEVEL OF LUCIDITY, IT IS IMPOSSIBLE FOR A PATHOLOGICAL POSSESSION TO BE INSTALLED BETWEEN TWO CONSCIOUSNESSES.

It is supposed, as a hypothesis – as has already been discussed – that the extraphysical parapopulation on Earth is 9 times greater than our intraphysical population. This always makes us ponder the extent of our evolutionary problem.

Interconsciential intrusion is currently humanity's biggest illness. This has been a fact for many millennia.

In many cases, through reunions, consciousnesses learn of the reality of the self-relay process involved in a personal task, which they have been executing over centuries, in many human bodies, different occupations, and multiple diverse intraphysical societies.

The more lucid and mature the consciousness, the broader is their global vision with respect to other consciousnesses, energies and the surrounding universe.

In this way, the consciousness who has gone through the deactivation of the human body, undergoes the second desoma or *second death* (deactivation of the energetic remnants of the holochakra) and returns to their original extraphysical condition.

THE SECOND DESOMA OF THE MORE LUCID CONSCIOUSNESS OCCURS WITHIN 3 TO 7 DAYS AFTER THE DEACTIVATION OF THE SOMA.

Obviously, the relative numbers of three to seven days correspond to the impression that we have in human life regarding the passage of chronological time.

Through a personal awareness of what is important within the most universalistic sense of fraternity, extraphysical consciousnesses identify and calculate their exact percentage of existential completism.

They evaluate what was previously planned in their life programming and what was in fact accomplished during the period they spent breathing among all of us, the components of humanity.

After some time of extraphysical confusion even the most mediocre or ordinary consciousness with regards to high priority knowledge of evolution, eventually ends up following the law of interconsciential affinities.

At this point, the consciousnesses naturally reach the exact extraphysical community where they came from before acquiring their recently discarded human body. This can occur through a type of *paratactility* as well as the influence of their consciential energies.

Back in the *extraphysical hometown*, they are once again together with their true peers, evolutionary partners with whom they have a closer and deeper affinity.

They reach a *maximum empathy* with others and ponder the results of the human life that has just ended.

They rejoice upon encountering old friends and suffer upon facing old antagonists. Joys and frustrations come to the surface.

Through the holomemory they remember the millenary past, temporarily forgotten by the inevitable consciential restriction of human existence.

Finally, when more lucid of their true *brand new-very old situation*, consciousnesses plan their upcoming experiential period.

At this point, a large number of more intimate consciential meetings may occur through extraphysical approaches.

What is an *extraphysical approach?*

AN EXTRAPHYSICAL APPROACH IS THE DIRECT CONTACT OF ONE CONSCIOUSNESS WITH ANOTHER IN DIMENSIONS OUTSIDE OF DENSE MATTER.

These approaches can be intentional or not and occur with or without lucidity between healthy consciousnesses, between pathological consciousnesses and also between a healthy and a sick consciousness.

When there is personal merit, not only do the helpers of the recently arrived consciousness intervene but the Evolutionologist exercising his evolved functions also intercedes and directs the consciousness to new paths, experiences and improved learning experiences.

During this opportunity for reevaluating human life, the consciousness can experience extraphysical euphoria or extraphysical melancholy.

What is *extraphysical euphoria?*

Extraphysical euphoria occurs after somatic deactivation and is generated by the reasonable execution of the existential program in the recently ended human life.

What is *extraphysical melancholy?*

Extraphysical melancholy is a postsomatic melancholy.

Consciousnesses orient themselves with respect to the extraphysical environment, millenary time, other consciousnesses closest to their intimate evolutionary group and – what is most relevant – their high priority personal and group tasks related to the dynamic development of their lucid evolution.

At this point, depending on our level of conscientiality, each one of us find ourselves as a *minipiece* (minicog), more or less conscientially active, within an *assistantial maxistructure* (maximechanism) between *consciousnesses* and between the *dimensions* in which we manifest.

In any religion, sect or line of mystical thought in which you participate, you must accept the full body of stratified theological doctrine that they impose.

IT IS USELESS TO TRY TO CHANGE ANY STRATIFIED DOCTRINE OR FOSSILIZING HOLOTHOSENE THAT IS STUCK IN TIME AS A RESULT OF DOGMAS.

This fact is as useless as getting on a train that is going in the direction opposite to the one you want to go and then trying to run back through the train cars in the other direction. The train will always take you inescapably backwards or at least cause you delays. This condition generates intraphysical and extraphysical melancholy.

One of the most striking consequences of *recalled extraphysical melancholy,* whether through preconscious *intuitions* or open and direct *healthy retrocognitions,* is the repudiation and distrust, in the intraphysical dimension, of all types of mystification, myths, mythologies, rituals, symbolism, superstitions, demagogisms, farces and parodies.

As a result of having succumbed to the tricks of imagination, sometimes more than once, the ego para-instinctively protects itself in an aggressive manner against all kinds of repression, folkloric influence, confabulation, mysticism, or manifestations that are distant from rationality, authenticity and frankness. The consciousness does this in order to avoid the repetition of mistakes in the establishment of their primary directives for living again (reliving) in matter.

The human tasks of destiny are chosen first according to the degree of the consciousness' liberation first from their egokarma and next from their groupkarma. The consciousness finally arrives at polykarmality.

ONLY A SMALL MINORITY OF THE COMPONENTS OF HUMANITY HAS ALREADY OPENED ITS EVOLVED POLYKARMIC ACCOUNT.

The consciousness performs a detailed analysis of three types of *personal manifestation*: accomplishments, mistakes and deficit-producing omissions. These deficit-producing omissions correspond to what the consciousness failed to do even though it was important and was programmed during the intermissive period.

We can not, therefore, be afraid of the *body's death* or of our immediate future after cremation of the soma.

We can identify the results of our life, today, right now. It is sufficient to evaluate what we have done so far.

There is no transcendent mystery involved in this context. Nor do we need to appeal to any special resource of our imagination.

We can free ourselves from all the transitory conditioning of human society in order to perform this evaluation.

We can execute, for example, a high level existential recycling and even participate in a group of existential recyclers.

What is a group of existential recyclers?

A group of existential recyclers is designed to promote intraphysical meetings and experiences together in a group scenario, aiming at the experience of planned existential recycling.

During the intermissive period, extraphysical consciousnesses *visit* environments and personalities they lived with and who are still in material life.

Many parapsychic phenomena occur with people who have suffered a temporary loss of their dearest human companions such as: spontaneous clairvoyance, abrupt apparitions and unforgettable extraphysical encounters.

There are millions and millions of occurrences wherein these people temporarily leave their bodies through conscious projections and meet their *deceased ex-relatives* in extraphysical communities that are closer to intraphysical life on Earth.

No consciousness profoundly changes their personality just because they lost their human body.

All intimate changes for the better regarding our temperament and the singular personality that we are, demand personal efforts, better performance and full awareness of what we do.

There are no dishonest favors or anticosmoethical privileges within the mechanism of the fundamental laws that rule the cosmos.

We are what we have built for ourselves.

We enjoy the happiness or the sadness that we ourselves have created.

We have within us our paradise or our hell.

Our cosmoethics unerringly calibrates our thosenes and our energies. The entirety of our energies situates each one of us, consciously or not, in a specific level in life, in any dimension, always.

We, ourselves, and no one else can make the *most profound changes*. The cosmos provides *anti-error mechanisms*.

While we are human intraphysical consciousnesses, and even while extraphysical without human bodies, if we exceed our personal rights to the detriment of the consciential rights of the others, or if we exceed our personal conditioned liberty, then the environment itself naturally and inevitably turns against us.

If this happens on Earth, it can result in an early desoma, *premature* cerebral death or a slow and unconscious suicide.

It can them be seen, for example, that the worst tyrant does not last for more than a few decades of despotism or truculence.

If changes do not occur in the paratropospheric extraphysical dimensions, an inexorable *energetic encapsulation* occurs through parapathological alterations of the holosoma.

The unstable, pathological and anticosmoethical energies of the extraphysical consciousness begin to disturb the formal stability of their psychosoma. This causes their manifestations to become unbalanced in a manner that is uncomfortable even to them, until an unbearable point is reached that demands unavoidable renovations and changes for the better.

At this threshold, the consciousness seeks other courses of action.

NO ONE CAN TAKE ANY PERSONAL CONSCIENTIAL ACCOMPLISHMENTS FROM ANOTHER. CONSCIOUSNESSES BLOCK THEMSELVES.

The more evolved the consciousnesses are, the more they value their own personal strong points and ours as well.

No personal effort is ever lost.

Everything is recorded in our integral memory.

What we have learned is never forgotten.

Is the effort in favor of our lucid evolution worthwhile or not?

Projective and parapsychic facts prove these assertions to any interested and motivated person who is not enslaved by *brainwashing* and preconceived ideas and who is not afraid of discovering their own greater reality.

Whoever has the following 4 things already has a certain notable level of discernment: good taste, good will, good intention and good humor.

13. EVOLUTIONARY TIES

Which companions most influence our evolution?

Within our evolutionary group, or groupkarma, the elements that most influence our personal or team evolution are our closest companions of destiny.

We can derive temporary benefits, advantages, or even enjoy human privileges from our evolutionary colleagues.

OUR ATTITUDES TOWARDS ONE ANOTHER EITHER *TIGHTEN* OR *LOOSEN* THE EVOLUTIONARY TIES IN OUR MUTUAL RELATIONSHIPS.

Ties of the most diverse nature strongly unite us.

First the affective ties, whether familial or not, are predominantly related to the psychosoma.

Next are cultural, intellectual ties or empathy, or those connections related to the mentalsoma.

Finally, there are links of social, commercial, industrial or professional interests concerning our human survival, which are related to all of our holosoma.

Our ties with one another create healthy or pathological effects. This occurs as a consequence of our still subhuman, conscious, semi-conscious or totally unconscious manifestations in a blind flight through the evolutionary process.

The healthy effects of our manifestations are liberating and evolutionary for us and for those we love, or those who are nearest and dearest to us in any dimension.

The pathological effects of our manifestations are stationary or regressive with respect to our evolution and the evolution of those we like and who live around us. An example of this is groupkarmic interprison.

Groupkarmic interprison, as previously discussed, is a life condition or a joint, compulsory, imposed and prolonged imprisonment among a group of antisocial and anticosmoethical consciousnesses.

Their existences and experiences are confined to each other by inseparable principles of intersciential affinities that act through their thosenes.

OUR ACHIEVEMENTS AND FAILURES ALWAYS UNITE US, ANYWHERE, IN ANY DIMENSION OR EVOLUTIONARY MOMENT.

Together we can either enjoy happy memories, exaltation, joy and euphoria or suffer sorrow, regret, tears and disappointment.

There are mutual and reciprocal intersciential prisons.

Our ties bind us like *tight shackles* or free us like *evolutionary keys*, opening wide the horizons of our immediate future. It all depends on the experience of maxifraternity.

During the phase of groupkarmic interprison, the consciousnesses, prisoners of one another, want to break away from each other but are unable to.

Yesterday's dearest colleague becomes today's most insensitive and implacable persecutor due to the irrationality of emotions.

The purest affection of the past becomes the declared and undisguisable hatred of the present.

They want to live apart because they, at least temporarily, can not stand each other. However, their common mistakes, executed at the same time, by four or by a hundred hands, prevail and impose the presence of one with the others.

Here you can ask:

And the helpers, in this case, don't they do anything?

The helpers do what they can, but they can not do the impossible. The so-called *extraphysical blind guides* are involved in these cases.

Each one of us thinks and decides for himself or herself. No one can live or decide for another, not even the helpers or the Evolutionologists.

The extraphysical helpers sponsor beneficent interconsciential semi-possessions. This demonstrates evolutionary *balance* on the part of lucid consciousnesses who are dedicated to maxifraternity

None of the more evolved consciousnesses will sponsor a pathological possession. This is the *madness* of the interconsciential intruder.

At the same time, no one can escape the effects of their own acts.

OUR INTEGRAL MEMORY REGISTERS EVERYTHING THAT WE DO, WITHOUT GAPS. THIS SERVES AS A TESTIMONY IN OUR FAVOR OR A DEPOSITION AGAINST US.

All of this functions like an automatic, inexorable and perpetually working instrument.

This is why we can affirm with absolute confidence that everything in the cosmos is under the control of more evolved intelligences or consciousnesses.

We do not need to torment ourselves over everything that we do not yet know. Nor should we suffer with terrifying expectations of the future or changes in epoch, paradigms, dimensions or evolutionary conditions.

Our level and quality of consciential energy automatically places us in affinity with and in the proximity of energies that are identical to those that we exteriorize and sustain.

Changes of dimensions and human bodies, moves to different intraphysical places or entries into different societies are not strong enough to separate us.

Likes attract each other with an irresistible force.

Nobody loses anybody. Nobody gets rid of anybody.

From a cosmoethical standpoint, therein lies the intelligence and advantage of doing what is most correct, both individually and in group, or in the midst of our evolutionary partners.

By getting things right, our acts impel us towards greater achievements and relationships with consciousnesses who are correct and healthier.

By erring, our actions propel us towards more mistakes and association with mistaken and sick consciousnesses.

This is the inevitable law of action and reaction that acts within us, intraconscientially, through our thosenes and energies and even against our will and intention.

To experience the reaction of our actions, there is no need for an inspector to observe the minutiae of our acts.

Our consciential energies are imperturbable in their insensitive, natural, machine-like judgments, within an incredibly impartial system of justice.

Our personal energies always disclose our level of evolutionary accomplishment.

Every pathological act results in an unhealthy backlash.

Every cosmoethical act results in an enriching return.

Many times we forget this reality because the return action is not immediate, although it is inevitable.

Nevertheless, the personal and non-transferable choice is ours.

*I*F WE CHOOSE TO ERR IN GROUP, WE RECEIVE, AS AN INEVITABLE RESPONSE, THE EFFECTS OF OUR ERRORS IN GROUPKARMIC INTERPRISON.

When consciousnesses begin to err in group – for example, the groups involved in the famous *social welfare scams* in Brazil – they become evolutionary delinquents.

They become members of the *intruder faction*.

They feel good in one another's company.

They happily conspire in a criminal climate with their anti-social companions.

For a period of time, they nurture *absolute certainties* regarding everything that they do wrong.

They feel they have the absolute right to infringe upon the rights of others.

However, the majority of these consciousnesses are very much aware of the *erroneous or spurious nature* of what they are doing.

They do not accept opportune warnings from people who are close to them or who are morally superior.

They persist in their transgressions, abuse their powers and sink into the mire without any reflection on the matter.

Many of these consciousnesses involve incautious companions, colleagues, spouses, children and relatives (nepotism) through heterocorruption and seduction consistent with the abuses of temporal, economic, social and political powers, and the powers of *theological empires*.

These abuses give rise to the spurious fruits of groupkarmic interprison, for instance: extermination groups, religious or political inquisitions; intergroupal human torture; racism and its madness; Mafias and criminal societies; terrorism; wars and genocide.

Groupkarmic interprison is based on the condition of evolutionary interconsciential inseparability.

What is *interconsciential inseparability?*

Interconsciential or evolutionary inseparability is the universal law of thosenic affinity: those who generate *identical thosenes* attract each other and live together in an inseparable fashion.

Consciousnesses only separate or temporarily distance themselves in order to lead new liberating, selfless group experiences, together with other consciousnesses.

As long as they stubbornly insist on committing selfish acts, they inexorably remain together, even against their will.

Errors are always yokes, shackles, castrating and paralyzing agents.

PERSONAL ACCOMPLISHMENTS ARE ALWAYS LIBERATIONS AND FREE FLIGHTS OF THE CONSCIOUSNESS INTO THE COSMOS AND CONTINUED EVOLUTION.

In order to leave the condition of groupkarmic interprison, consciousnesses undergo several phases until they achieve emancipation from the web of delinquent ties that they have imposed on themselves and in which they became ensnared.

In the beginning, they pass through the victimization phase.

What is the victimization phase?

In the victimization phase the delinquent consciousnesses, deserters of lucid evolution, begin to doubt the advantages of their actions and less dignified choices.

Losing strength, they start to feel *first hand* the repercussion of their erroneous actions.

They lose their transitory power, can be ostracized, become isolated by society and receive pressure from all sides.

From a position of leadership, these consciousnesses become victims of the same *antisocial machine* they helped to create and operate.

This period of *payback* depends on the effects of their actions when they worked in the antisocial team, and can take several centuries and many human lives of full-time dedication to the betterment of the *unbreathable environment* that they created.

This is when they sacrifice themselves in favor of their colleagues and the victims of their actions in order to be able to live in peace with themselves and others.

PROFOUND CHANGES IN PERSONALITY REQUIRE ALTERATIONS OF WILL, INTENTION AND ORGANIZATION OF PERSONAL HABITS.

This effort, with time, involves the establishment of new synapses in the cerebral hemispheres that are related to newly incorporated ideas.

In this way consciousnesses progress one way or another, until they reach the recomposition phase.

What is the recomposition phase?

The recomposition phase is that in which the consciousnesses who erred in group cease to be *direct victims* of their mistakes in order to attend to the needs of their *former victims*.

Little by little, with great effort, patience and perseverance, usually in the same environment, country or society, with the same egos or *mega-egos in new somas*, consciousnesses reassemble the pieces and wreckage of anything useful that is left over from their abuses.

DURING THE RECOMPOSITION PHASE OF THE EVOLUTIONARY PROCESS, ALL OF THE CONSCIOUSNESS' EFFORTS GO WRONG.

Who does not know people immersed in the recomposition phase?

These are those men and women who complain incessantly: "Nothing in my life works out! Everything is against me! I have been forgotten by destiny!"

During this recomposition phase, consciousnesses try to *unteach whatever they taught wrong*, until they liberate themselves from their own foolishness, inexperience and clamorous mistakes.

After the recomposition phase comes the liberation phase, wherein the consciousnesses feel relieved of intrusive pressures, even when these pressures are centennial or multi-existential.

They discard infantile egocentrism, acquire a better sense of humanity and no longer constantly asks for themselves.

They discover polykarma and help others without thinking of themselves, without asking for gratitude or reward, with the exclusive objective of comfortable and joint evolution.

For these consciousnesses, Earth becomes an evolutionary school.

They want to learn together with others.

They want to teach while learning in group.

They want to succeed together with others, instead of erring in group.

They want to show that they have learned the evolutionary lesson.

At this point, they discover universalism, above and beyond all sectarian doctrines, individualistic philosophies, beliefs, sanctification, repression, and *brainwashing.*

The day arrives when they recognize the existence of the clarification task as being much more important than the consolation task.

They begin to defend themselves against blind intrudability through applied cosmoethics.

They arrive at a more tranquil plateau of holomaturity.

WITH TIME AND NEW EXPERIENCES, EACH ONE OF US IMPROVES OUR PERSONAL HOLOTHOSENE WITHIN THE GROUP HOLOTHOSENE.

14. CYCLE OF LIVES
OF THE CONSCIOUSNESS

What is the *multi-existential cycle?*

At our average evolutionary level, the multi-existential cycle is a system of continuously alternating existential states, composed of a period of human life (intraphysical rebirth) and another extraphysical period (deactivation of the soma), which takes the consciousness into the intermissive phase. These two periods constitute the set of the consciousness' incessant *evolutionary itinerary.*

Each consciousness can always be in 1 of 3 states: the *extraphysical* state or of their true dimension; the *intraphysical* state of transitory human life; and the fleeting *projected* state, characteristic of both intraphysical and extraphysical consciousnesses when they project.

The interval between one human life and the next, as already addressed, constitutes the intermissive period, during which intermissive courses can take place.

HUMAN CALENDARS DO NOT SERIOUSLY INFLUENCE THE CRITERIA THAT RULE OUR MULTI-EXISTENTIAL CYCLES.

Here, we pose an intelligent and opportune question:

On a scale from 1 to 5, at what polykarmic stage do you place yourself today?

Depending on the condition of the extraphysical consciousnesses, whether they are free from major karmic commitments or immersed in some stage of their groupkarmic interprison, they invariably embark on liberating extraphysical experiences and research.

Otherwise, they will compulsorily return, sooner or later, into a new human body, and to new reformative experiences in intraphysical life.

When lucid and in possession of personal merit, consciousnesses are advised to compose, with all available lucidity, their extraphysical agenda.

What is *an extraphysical agenda?*

An extraphysical agenda is the set of data laid out in an intelligent plan, through which a consciousness organizes their studies, investigations and research during the intermissive period.

THE EXTRAPHYSICAL AGENDA INVOLVES ALL OF THE MOST EVOLVED CONSCIENTIAL RESOURCES AND ATTRIBUTES OF THE CONSCIOUSNESS' MENTALSOMA.

For this task, the consciousness will employ, for instance, the holomemory, the most remote retrocognitions, intra-consciential associations of logical ideas, elevated sentiments and personal energies. This is done within the most evolved *thosenology* possible.

Veteran human conscious projectors *imitate* the extraphysical agendas of extraphysical consciousnesses in order to develop their performance, psychic capacities, extracorporeal abilities and experiences, thus constituting the familiar *agenda of the projected projector.*

The projector's agenda contains a written list of high priority extraphysical consciential targets – beings, places, ideas – that the projector endeavors to gradually reach, in a chronological manner, establishing *intelligent schemes* for his or her development.

Through the data entered in the agenda, the extraphysical consciousness can arrive at a primary or advanced intermissive course, *after* the second desoma and *before* the new human life.

The extraphysical consciousness can then go through several extraphysical stages in preparation for the new human life.

A new minutely planned existential program can then be delineated after visiting planets other than Earth on learning excursions with *flying groups*. These learning excursions aim to greatly amplify the consciousnesses' approach with respect to the evolution that is to be achieved in the intimacy of the evolutionary group, which is inevitable.

DEPENDING ON THEIR LEVEL OF CONSCIENTIALITY, EXTRAPHYSICAL CONSCIOUSNESSES HAVE AN INTERVIEW WITH THE EVOLUTIONOLOGIST OF THEIR KARMIC GROUP.

The Evolutionologist ends up informing the consciousnesses of their specific multi-existential cycle. This, consequently, generates a very pertinent question:

At what point are you in your *multi-existential cycle?*

The Evolutionologist can identify the exact stage of consciousnesses within their multi-existential cycle, or in the cyclic frequency of their intraphysical lives, the criteria of which obey multiple variables.

We are going to analyze, for example, 3 criteria of multi-existential cycles: groupkarmality, complementarity, and activity.

What is *groupkarmality* within the criteria of the multi-existential cycle?

The criterion of groupkarmality is based on the consciousnesses' groupkarmic account, wherein the *groupal* karmic debt is greater than the *personal* karmic debt.

In this case the duration of the *human* life and the duration of the *intermissive* life, between one physical lifetime and the next, depend, over a long evolutionary stretch, on the consciousness' personal debts in intimate relation to the debts of the closest components of the evolutionary group.

In short: the multi-existential cycle of your evolutionary group determines your personal multi-existential cycle.

This criterion includes countless consanguine human lives, that is, consciousnesses who repeatedly participate in *diverse branches of the same genealogical tree.*

This criterion also encompasses the consciousnesses with very restricted levels of individualization and the participants in collective madness; for instance, group suicides, such as those that took place with the religious fanatics in British Guiana.

Another criterion is that of complementarity.

What is *complementarity* within the criteria of the multi-existential cycle?

The criterion of complementarity involves consciousnesses who directly, in a single instance, or indirectly, in a chronic fashion, committed suicide and were immediately reborn after their insane act in order to complement the human period that was previously planned but not lived.

In this way, consciousnesses who committed suicide benefit from the opportunity of living together again with the consciousnesses that they left behind, about whom they did not think and whose conviviality and assistance they need.

CONSCIOUSNESSES WHO COMMIT SUICIDE TEND TO REDUCE THEIR EXTRAPHYSICAL OR INTERMISSIVE PERIODS OVER A LONG STRETCH OF THEIR EVOLUTIONARY PATH.

A third criterion is activity.

What is *activity* within the criteria of the multi-existential cycle?

The criterion of activity within the multi-existential cycle is applied according to the demands of the multi-existential liberating activities of more lucid consciousnesses who wish to realize accomplishments beyond those of the evolutionary middle class.

They aspire to become a more and more lucid and efficient *minicog* within the assistantial *maximechanism* or assistantial structure between consciousnesses.

They want to forget their millenary mega-ego and strive for new evolutionary conquests that are more valid and much more comfortable in other consciential dimensions.

In this case, the periods of human life, as well as the intermissive periods, no longer depend on the will of the consciousness, or on their conscious free will. These periods can vary greatly and are independent of each other.

LUCID CONSCIOUSNESSES TRUST THE GIANTS OF EVOLUTION AHEAD OF THEM: EVOLUTIONOLOGISTS, SERENISSIMUS AND FREE CONSCIOUSNESSES.

These are the leaders of the maximechanism dedicated to assistantiality with whom the lucid consciousness directly or indirectly relates all the time.

Lucid consciousnesses allow their destiny to be resolved together with these leaders in evolution, within the holothosene of assistantial, evolutionary work, shoulder to shoulder and hand in hand.

They accept with satisfaction whatever is best for everyone, over their own pretensions and old selfishness.

A tendency spontaneously arises for their intermissive periods to become progressively more extensive.

The necessity for imposed human life diminishes for consciousnesses who are now more lucid and self-aware.

A life of human leadership sometimes demands continuous extraphysical assistance or excellence in one's intermissive work over a long polykarmic period. For example, this is the case when a consciousness acts as an extraphysical helper for needy intraphysical consciousnesses.

Consciousnesses then start to grasp what they did not understand when they were receiving the helpers' dedicated assistance over the long series of their successive lives.

Do you find consistency, rationality and logic in these 3 criteria for the multi-existential cycles?

Evidently, many other criteria exist for the establishment of our multi-existential cycles, but these 3 are the most accessible and the ones which are most important within our currently reduced evolutionary discernment.

We all must progress, with lucidity and intentionality, as soon as possible, towards the criterion of interconsciential assistantial activity.

CONSCIOUSNESSES WHO BECOME PERMANENTLY-TOTALLY-INTRUSION-FREE TEND TOWARDS THE MULTI-EXISTENTIAL CYCLE OF ACTIVITY.

Do you think that you are already oriented by the criterion of activity in your multi-existential cycle?

The criterion of activity within the multi-existential cycle leads the consciousness to first discover the achievement of the permanently-totally-intrusion-free condition, and later, the world of consciential serenism.

15. EVOLUTION OF THE CONSCIOUSNESS

Have you been able to follow the stages of *our evolution* so far?

Starting with the period prior to acquiring a human body, going through the phases of physical life, we arrive at the extraphysical study of the multi-existential cycle, wherein consciousnesses completing their cycle – *extraphysical life, intraphysical life, extraphysical life* – again face the possibility of re-acquiring a new physical body.

Let us now perform an overall or panoramic analysis of everything that is best for us in order to confront the stages that we are all subjected to, with their inevitable challenges and difficulties.

ONE FUNDAMENTAL AND UNDISPUTED POINT EXISTS: WITHOUT HELPING OTHERS, WE WILL NEVER ACCELERATE OUR PERSONAL EVOLUTION.

This is a point that dispenses with any major discussion among *paraphilosophers* and veteran conscious projectors.

Lucid projectors have, in this existence, already experienced what life will be like after the deactivation of the human body. We can consider them to be among those personalities most capable of giving a qualified opinion regarding these paramount issues that concern us all.

Irrespective of who he is, unfortunately, the common philosopher is a mere *theoretician* if he has not been able to temporarily leave the soma and experience the realities of his *consciential extraphysical hometown*.

Conclusion: applied fraternity is unavoidable and irreplaceable for all of us.

What is *maxifraternity?*

Maxifraternity is the universalistic, more evolved interconsciential condition, founded on the pure fraternity of consciousnesses who are *self-unforgiving* (do not forgive their own errors) and *hetero-forgiving* (always forgive the mistakes of others). This is an inevitable goal in the evolution of all consciousnesses. To forgive is to comprehend while helping.

MAXIFRATERNITY MAKES IT POSSIBLE FOR THE HUMAN CONSCIOUSNESS TO EXPERIENCE THE IMPACTFUL PHENOMENON OF COSMOCONSCIOUSNESS.

Nobody evolves without voluntarily and consciously serving others.

What is *cosmoconsciousness?*

Cosmoconsciousness is the condition or inner perception of the consciousness with respect to the cosmos, life and the order of the universe, in a state of intellectual and cosmoethical exaltation that is impossible to describe, in which the consciousness senses the living presence of the universe and becomes one with it, temporarily composing an indivisible unity.

What is most important during the phenomenon of cosmoconsciousness is the occurrence of *interconsciential communication* with more evolved beings. This allows retrocognitions and intimate enlightenment to occur that are based in logic, rationality and discernment.

After experiencing the phenomenon of cosmoconsciousness, which is produced through the lucid projection of the mentalsoma, the projector seeks out evolved principles of inner liberation within advanced specialized human institutions, or conscientiocentric institutions.

What *is a conscientiocentric institution?*

A conscientiocentric institution centralizes its objectives on the consciousness, concentrating on consciential evolution in the manner of a *consciential cooperative*, within conscientiological human society, based on both the employment bond and the consciential bond.

The International Institute of Projectiology and Conscientiology, since its foundation, has had the intention of being a conscientiocentric institution.

The IIPC emphasizes the consciential bond and concerns itself with the elimination of all repression over its volunteers, researchers, teachers, and students.

This is why the following inscription of the *antibrainwashing technique* is strategically posted at all IIPC offices worldwide: "Don't believe in anyone or anything, not even the information you receive here at the Institute. Experiment. Have your own experiences."

In a conscientiocentric enterprise, the self-lucid, voluntary and polykarmic *consciential bond*, as a result of being more evolved, completely predominates over the common employment bond.

The existence of conscientiocentric institutions evidences that we have begun to live in the early dawn of this planet's consciential era. They reaffirm that this era is possible, attainable and practical in spite of the millenary clamoring of chronic pessimists.

What is the *consciential era?*

In the consciential era, the average intraphysical consciousness will be sufficiently evolved through the impacts, redefinitions and healthy revolutions created by multidimensional experience, or the voluntary and deliberate production of lucid projections of the consciousness that allow the human personality to visit and research evolved extraphysical communities.

Another name for our current evolutionary period is the *age of Serenissimus.* The Serenissimus is situated, in the evolutionary hierarchy, beyond the preserenissimus, the permanently-totally-intrusion-free and the Evolutionologist.

What is *preserenissimus?*

THE PRESERENISSIMUS IS AN INTRAPHYSICAL CONSCIOUSNESS, LIKE YOU AND I, OR AN EXTRAPHYSICAL CONSCIOUSNESS WHO IS STILL NOT ABLE TO ENJOY THE FULL CONDITION OF LUCID SERENITY.

We are on the path to serenism, but we are not there yet.

WHICH TAKES LONGER: FOR AN INFERIOR SUBHUMAN ANIMAL TO BECOME A PRESERENISSIMUS, OR FOR A PRESERENISSIMUS TO BECOME A SERENISSIMUS?

Without the shadow of a doubt, in this case, logic recommends the law of ascendance of the greater over the lesser.

In this context, the inferior subhuman animal takes longer to reach the evolutionary level of preserenissimus.

The more potentialities the consciousness already has, the greater will be the possibilities for reaching consciential expansion.

The taxonomy or the evolutionary classification of animals will always be precarious if analyzed solely from a human viewpoint. In order to more closely approximate evolutionary reality, taxonomy needs to be developed based on the holosoma of animals and in view of the alternating condition of the multidimensionality of consciential principles.

What is a *permanently-totally-intrusion-free being?*

A permanently-totally-intrusion-free being is a physical person – man or woman – who is completely self-aware of his or her permanently-totally-intrusion-free condition. He or she immediately detects, anytime and anywhere the presence of intruding consciousnesses and neither becomes involved nor disturbed by their pathological, intrusive actions. These intruding intraphysical or extraphysical consciousnesses may either be lucid (calculating and bad intentioned) or unconscious (postsomatic parapsychotics or *cannon fodder*).

THE PERMANENTLY-TOTALLY-INTRUSION-FREE INDIVIDUAL IS NO LONGER A VICTIM OF PERTURBING CONSCIOUSNESSES. TOGETHER WITH THE HELPERS, THEY SKILFULLY ASSIST THESE CONSCIOUSNESSES.

The permanently-totally-intrusion-free consciousness acts as conscious assistantial bait between consciential micro-universes.

Note: unfortunately, the absolute majority of human beings have not yet attained this evolved level of interconsciential *performance*; not even Nobel Prize laureate scientists, self-deifying sectarian religious leaders, artists of all kinds, health professionals in general (the biggest victims), and obviously the common people or the elements of the unthinking human masses.

It is obvious that permanently-totally-intrusion-free consciousnesses are always interested in all assistance that helpers and Evolutionologists perform.

What is *Serenissimus?*

Serenissimus is the popular name for *Homo sapiens serenissimus*, that consciousness who already integrally lives in the condition of lucid serenism.

Within the evolutionary hierarchy, *Homo sapiens serenissimus* is situated above Evolutionologists.

Serenism presents an *extreme paradox* at a certain level of its development: when you possess the highest level of impactful relative truth that you personally achieved in intraphysical life and have the best possible means of disseminating it to humankind, there will be significant cosmoethical impossibilities involved in using them.

This shows that the Serenissimus' condition of anonymity is not, in fact, totally chosen by them. Strictly speaking, a Serenissimus does not have a more intelligent or cosmoethical option other than anonymity.

The disclosure of certain levels of advanced knowledge can be more harmful than beneficial. This characterizes the anticosmoethical *evolutionary rape.*

This fact speaks in favor of the inevitable discriminatory nature of consciential evolution, everywhere, at all levels, moving nonetheless towards maxifraternity.

Fortunately or unfortunately, the hierarchy of evolution is based on frank elitism, whether we like it or not.

As a result of being in the last stages of physical experience through human, biological bodies (macrosomas), the Serenissimus is headed towards the *third desoma* or the deactivation of the *psychosoma,* which will initiate their mentalsomatic cycle.

What is the mentalsomatic cycle?

The mentalsomatic cycle is the *evolutionary course* of the consciousness who has already definitively deactivated the psychosoma and lives exclusively with the mentalsoma, existing as a free consciousness.

What is a *free consciousness?*

A free consciousness is that consciousness who has definitively discarded the *psychosoma* (emotional body). As a consequence, a free consciousness has also discarded the long string of intraphysical lives, equal to ours, in which we employ an energetic body *(holochakra)* and a human body *(soma).*

We are beings who are aware of our consciousness.

So far, we are the only terrestrial beings who recognize that we are conscious, lucid of ourselves. We ask: "Who am I? What is consciousness?"

We are capable of stopping and reflecting on our experiments.

We can change the world, as no other known intraphysical being has so far been able to.

Each one of us knows what it means to be conscious.

FREE CONSCIOUSNESS, WITHIN THE INEVITABLE EVOLUTIONARY HIERARCHY, IS LOCATED ABOVE HOMO SAPIENS SERENISSIMUS.

Lastly, we consider that we have been able to reasonably and logically answer the fundamental questions presented at the beginning of this book. They were:

Who are you?

You are an individual consciousness, a veritable micro-universe different from all others, with invaluable productive and evolutionary potentialities.

What are you?

You are an indestructible and extremely complex reality that must be studied above all by yourself.

Where did you come from?

You came from an extraphysical community of extraphysical consciousnesses that corresponds to your evolutionary level, where you were before acquiring your current temporary human body.

What are you doing in this life on Earth?

You seek to evolve by understanding the universe and developing a mastery of yourself and of things by employing the resources of human or material life.

Where are you going?

YOU WILL RETURN TO YOUR EXTRAPHYSICAL HOMETOWN IN ORDER TO UPDATE YOUR EVOLUTIONARY FILE AFTER THE DEACTIVATION OF THE PHYSICAL BODY.

This author invites even the most intransigent adversaries of the leading-edge relative truths discussed in this volume –

especially the cohesive and coherent principles of the science of conscientiology – as well as all those who are still not able to produce lucid projections of the consciousness on their own, to give a more logical, rational and detailed solution to the great evolutionary problems of humankind that are addressed herein.

All books merely function as sources of information.

ANY RENEWING CONCLUSION OR DECISION SHOULD ONLY BE PUT INTO PRACTICE AFTER DIRECT PERSONAL EXPERIENCE.

GLOSSARY OF CONSCIENTIOLOGY

Abdominal sub-brain – The umbilicalchakra (center of consciential energy located above the navel), when unconsciously selected by an intraphysical consciousness, of mediocre evolution, as the basis of their manifestations. The belly-brain, gutbrain, abdominal brain, abdominal pseudo-brain, or abdominal sub-brain, is a parody of the natural, encephalic brain (coronalchakra and frontalchakra); an indefensible embarrassment in conscious self-evolution.

Admiration-disagreement binomial – Binomial attributed to an intraphysical consciousness, evolutionarily mature, who already knows how to live in a peaceful coexistence with another intraphysical consciousness whom he or she loves and admires, but with whose points of view, opinions, and courses of action, they do not always 100% agree.

Advanced existential program – Existential program of an intraphysical consciousness who is an evolutionary leader, performing within a specific libertarian groupkarmic task that is more universalist and polykarmic in nature. This individual serves as a lucid, minicog acting within a maximechanism of a multidimensional team.

Altered state of consciousness – Any modification of the normal state of consciousness or awareness – such as sleep and drowsiness. It also includes states created by the use of drugs, hypnosis, or techniques of meditation. Recently also referred to as non-ordinary state of consciousness.

Alternating intraphysical preserenissimus – Intraphysical consciousness who is capable from time-to-time of simultaneously living consciously in the waking state as well as projected in the extraphysical dimensions.

Androchakra (*andro* + *chakra*) – Sexchakra of a man.

Androsoma (*andro* + *soma*) – Male human body, or soma specific to a man.

Androthosene (*composed word: andro* + *tho* + *sen* + *ene*) – Thosene of the primitive male or macho man.

Animism (*Latin: animus, soul*) – Set of intra and extracorporeal phenomena produced by the intraphysical consciousness without external interference. For example, the phenomenon of conscious projection induced by one's own will.

Antithosene (*anti* + *tho* + *sen* + *ene*) – Antagonistic thosene, common in refutations, omniquestionings, and in productive debates.

Aphrodisiac female sexsoma – A woman's soma, considered specifically in relation to its sex, when its appearance is able to work as an aphrodisiac. See gynosoma.

Artifacts of knowledge – Intellectual tools; resources used by the consciousness to store, retrieve or process information, such as books, computers and the internet.

Assistantiality - Related to or denoting assistance. An assistantial task is universalistic, cosmoethical, fraternal and should ideally be clarifying (clarification task) rather than consoling (consolation task).

Assisted conscious projection – Projection wherein a consciousness is directly assisted by a helper who is almost always an expert in lucid projectability.

Auric coupling – Interfusion of the holochakral energies between 2 or more consciousnesses.

Belly-brain – Same as abdominal sub-brain.

Biothosene (*bio* + *tho* + *sen* + *ene*) – Thosene specifically related to the human consciousness.

Bithanatose – Deactivation and discard of the holochakra after the first desoma, including the detachment of the remaining holochakral energetic connections in the psychosoma; second death, second desoma.

Blind guide – Inexperienced or amoral consciousness who helps another consciousness in detriment to others in an anticosmoethical manner, according to their momentary egotistic interests.

Bradythosene (*brady* + *tho* + *sen* + *ene*) – Thosene having a sluggish flow, pertaining to the slow-minded human consciousness.

Cardiochakra (*cardio* + *chakra*) – The fourth basic chakra; influential agent in the emotionality of an intraphysical consciousness. Vitalizes the heart and lungs. Also known as heart chakra.

Chakra – A nucleus or defined field of consciential energy. The totality of the many chakras in one's energetic system constitutes the holochakra or energetic parabody. The holochakra forms a junction between the soma and psychosoma, acting as a point of connection through which consciential energy flows from one vehicle to the other.

Chirosoma (*chiro* + *soma*) – The body considered specifically in regards to the use of hands or manual work.

Clarification task – Advanced assistantial task of elucidation or clarification that can be performed individually or in group. The clarification task promotes long-lasting evolutionary effects, as opposed to the short-term, immediate effects of the consolation task.

Con – Hypothetical unit of measurement of lucidity of an intraphysical or extraphysical consciousness.

Confor (*con* + *for*) – Synergy of content (idea, essence) with form (appearance, language) in the interconsciential communication processes (communicology).

Conscientese – Telepathic non-symbolic idiom that is native to the consciential dimensions of very evolved extraphysical societies.

Consciential amentia – Condition in which a consciousness is incapable of thinking with reasonable mental balance.

Consciential basement – Phase of infantile and adolescent manifestations of the intraphysical consciousness up until adulthood, characterized by a predominance of the more primitive weak traits of the consciousness.

Consciential bond – Cosmoethical, lucid, voluntary and polykarmic link between a person and an institution. The consciential bond goes beyond the employment bond.

Consciential co-epicenter – Helper who works with an intraphysical consciousness who is a veteran consciential epicenter during his or her personal energetic task (penta). This helper can work as a colleague in the daily practices of penta as well as in the constant assistance of extraphysical consciousnesses gathered in the epicenter's extraphysical assistantial facility.

Consciential concentration – The direct, unswerving, focusing of one's senses, consciential attributes, will, and intention upon a singular object.

Consciential continuism – Condition of wholeness in the continuity of consciential life - without gaps. This condition is possible through opportune and constructive forecast and evolutionary self-relay. In other words, the incessant connection of one's experiences of the present moment to those immediately before and after, in a cohesive and unified whole, without loss of continuity or empty consciential experiences.

Consciential ectopia – Unsatisfactory execution of one's existential program in an eccentric, dislocated manner, outside the programming chosen for the individual's intraphysical life.

Consciential energy – Immanent energy that a consciousness employs in their general manifestations; the ene of thosene; personal energy.

Consciential epicenter – Key intraphysical consciousness who becomes a fulcrum of interdimensional lucidity, assistantiality and constructiveness through the use of the extraphysical assistantial facility. Directly related to the penta or personal energetic task.

Consciential era – Era in which the average intraphysical consciousness finds themselves sufficiently evolved, through impacts, personal redefinition and revolutions created through their lucid projectability, implanting the sublimity of self-conscientiality.

Consciential eunuch – Individual conscientially castrated and manipulated by sectarians, domesticaters of satisfied human automatons (robots), modern slaves of the unthinking masses.

Consciential gestation – Evolutionary productivity on the part of an intraphysical consciousness in terms of the execution of their existential program.

Consciential hyperspace – Extraphysical consciential dimensions.

Consciential micro-universe – Consciousness when considered as a whole, including all of the attributes, thosenes and manifestations in their evolution. The microcosmos of the consciousness in relation to the macrocosmos of the universe.

Consciential monoendowment– Intraphysical life under the pressure of constant intrusions by ill beings. This is experienced by the ordinary intraphysical consciousnesses having few talents and no versatility.

Consciential paracomatose – State of extraphysical coma of a projected intraphysical consciousness, who invariably remains unconscious and, therefore, has no recall of extraphysical events.

Consciential paradigm – Leading-theory of conscientiology, founded in the consciousness itself.

Consciential restriction – Restriction of the consciousness due to the process of manifestation in the physical state, in which one's natural level of awareness is reduced.

Consciential retailing – A rudimentary system of individual behavior characterized by lesser, isolated consciential actions having a minimum of productive results or important evolutionary effects.

Consciential scaffolds – Dispensable psychological or physical aids or means used by the consciousness.

Consciential self-bilocation (*Latin: bis, two; and locus, place*) – Act whereby an intraphysical projector encounters and contemplates their own human body (soma) face-to-face, when their consciousness is outside of the soma, in another vehicle of consciential manifestation.

Consciential triendowment – Quality of the 3 conjugated talents most useful to a conscientiologist – intellectuality, paranormal abilities and communicability.

Consciential wholesaling – Behavior of an individual characterized by a tendency to approach issues in a comprehensive or wholesale manner so as not to leave negative evolutionary loose ends or gaps behind.

Conscientiocentric institution – Institution which centralizes its objectives on the consciousness and its evolution, as is the case with the International Institute of Projectiology and Conscientiology (IIPC); consciential cooperative within the Conscientiological Society, having employment and consciential bonds at its foundation.

Conscientiocentrism – Social philosophy that concentrates its objectives in the consciousness per se and in its evolution. Conscientiocentrism is a subject covered by conscientiocentrology, the area of conscientiology which studies the establishment and maintenance of a conscientiocentric institution based on consciential and employment bonds – like a consciential cooperative – in the conscientiological intraphysical society.

Conscientiogram – Technical plan for measuring the evolutionary level of the consciousness; consciential megatest having the *Homo sapiens serenissimus* as a model – Serenissimus being responsible for a positive egokarmic account. The conscientiogram is the basic instrument employed in conscientiometric tests.

Conscientiologist – Intraphysical consciousness engaged in the continuing study and objective experimentation in the field of conscientiological research. The conscientiologist operates as an agent of evolutionary renovation (retrocognitive agent), in the liberating work of consciousnesses in general.

Conscientiology – Science that studies consciousnesses in an integral, holosomatic, multidimensional, multimillenary, multiexistential manner and above all, according to their reactions with regards to immanent energy, consciential energy, and their own multiple states of being.

Conscious projection (CP) – Projection of an intraphysical consciousness beyond the soma; extracorporeal experience; out-of-body experience (OBE). The phenomenon of the conscious projection also encompasses the case where extraphysical consciousnesses achieve lucid departures from the psychosoma manifesting themselves through the mentalsoma.

Consciousness, the – The individual essence or intelligent principle in constant evolution. In conscientiology the word consciousness (as in "the consciousness") is considered to be synonymous with mind, ego, intelligent principle, etc., and is not being used to refer to a state of consciousness. Outworn synonyms: soul, spirit.

Consolation task – An elementary-level personal or group assistantial task of consolation.

Co-projector – Helper who works in conjunction with an intraphysical consciousness during the realization of lucid, assisted consciential projections.

Coronalchakra (*coronal* + *chakra*) – Chakra at the top of the head, crowning the holochakra; crown chakra.

Cosmoconsciousness – Condition or perception of the inner consciousness of the cosmos, of life and order of the universe, in an intellectual and cosmoethical exaltation that is impossible to describe. In this case, a consciousness senses the living presence of the universe and becomes one with it, in an indivisible unit. Interconsciential communication occurs in this extraordinary condition.

Cosmoethical mimicry – Productive social impulse towards imitation of one's evolved forebears (such as the consciential gestations performed in previous lives).

Cosmoethicality – The cosmoethical nature of a consciousness.

Cosmoethics – Ethics or reflection over the cosmic, multidimensional morality, or the cosmic moral that defines consciential holomaturity. Cosmoethics goes beyond the social, intraphysical moral or the moral presented under human labels. It arises from the intimacy of one's consciential micro-universe as maximal, moral and emotional discernment.

Cosmothosene (*cosmo* + *tho* + *sen* + *ene*) – Thosene specifically related to conscientese or the state of cosmoconsciousness; form of communication of conscientese.

Co-therapist – Helper who works with an intraphysical consciousness who is the therapist while a patient is being treated. It occurs during the assistantial technical procedures of conscientiotherapy.

Co-thosene (*co* + *tho* + *sen* + *ene*) – Thosene specifically related to the collective actions of a chorus, of those praying in groups or crowds.

Counterbody – Same as holochakra, the vehicle of the consciential energy of an intraphysical consciousness; energetic body.

Counterthosene (*counter* + *tho* + *sen* + *ene*) – Intraconsciential thosene of an intraphysical consciousness; mute mental refutation; mental word; mute thosene; a type of *intrathosene*.

Cryptothosene – Unit of measurement of daydreaming.

Daydream – Fanciful story created by one's imagination during the waking state of the human consciousness.

Dermatologies of the consciousness – Compound expression attributed to the conventional, physicalist sciences that are subordinated to the newtonian-cartesian, mechanistic paradigm, and focus their research only on the soma – not availing themselves of the instrumentation necessary for the direct, technical investigation of the consciousness itself; dermatological (superficial) approaches to the consciousness. Periconsciential sciences.

Desoma (*de* + *soma*) – Somatic deactivation, impending and inevitable for all intraphysical consciousnesses; final projection; first death; biological death; monothanatosis. Desoma is the deactivation of a soma or body. First desoma, or simply desoma, is the deactivation of the human body (physical death). Second desoma is the deactivation of the holochakra. Third desoma is the deactivation of the psychosoma.

Destructive macro-PK – Harmful PK (psychokinesis) capable of causing injuries to the intraphysical consciousness. Destructive macro-PK can prove fatal.

Domiciliary holothosene – Physical base; bedroom that has been energetically shielded; extraphysical assistantial facility.

Doxothosene – Unit of measurement of the principles of the consciousness (holomaturology).

Dream – Natural consciential state that is intermediary between the waking state and natural sleep. Dreams are characterized by a set of ideas and images that present themselves to the consciousness. An afflictive dream includes agitation, anguish and oppression in its development, and is known as: nightmare; night terror; nightmarish hallucination.

Egokarma (*ego* + *karma*) – Principle of cause and effect acting in the evolution of the consciousness, when centered exclusively around the ego per se. State wherein one's free will is restricted by infantile egocentrism.

Egothosene (*ego* + *tho* + *sen* + *ene*) – Same as self-thosene; unit of measurement of consciential egotism according to conscientiology or, more appropriately, according to conscientiometry.

Energetic dimension – Energetic dimension of the consciousnesses; holochakral dimension; three-and-a-half dimension. Dimension natural to the holochakra.

Energetic intrusion – Invasion of an intraphysical consciousness by another using consciential energies or the holochakra; holochakral intrusion.

Energetic maxispringtime – Condition of a maximized or prolonged energetic springtime (energetic plenitude).

Energetic minispringtime – Condition of a minimal or ephemeral energetic springtime (energetic plenitude).

Energetic springtime – A more-or-less long-lasting condition wherein one's consciential energies exhibit an optimal, healthy, constructive profile.

Energetic springtime by two – Energetic springtime of an evolutionary duo, the partners of which truly love each other and have mastered the application of healthy consciential energy with complete lucidity, building their existential program through consciential gestations.

Energyvorous – Energy consuming, energy draining; in reference to intruder(s).

Enumerology – Didactic technique of processing texts based on informative self-scrutiny.

Evolutionary duo – Two consciousnesses that interact positively in joint evolution; existential condi-tion of cooperative evolutionality by two individuals who are committed to each other's evolutionary progress.

Evolutionary orientor – See Evolutionologist.

Evolutionologist – Consciousness who assists in the intelligent coordination of an individual's existential program or in the consciential evolution of one or more consciousnesses of the groupkarma. Evolutionary condition in-between *Serenissimus* and the state of being completely and permanently intrusion free. Synonym: evolutionary orientor.

Exception-conduct – Atypical, ectopic or dislocated pattern of behavior.

Existential completism – Condition of a human consciousness upon completing their existential program.

Existential incompletism – Condition wherein the existential program of a human consciousness is incomplete.

Existential inversion – It is the highest degree of technical planning of the human life that an intraphysical consciousness is capable of performing based on conscientiology and Projectiology. This planning is performed without any doctrinarian, sectarian, inculcating, mystical, or even academic/scientific influences. It is based on prioritization and the full time conscious dedication to the execution of one's existential program since puberty or at the latest before the age of 26.

Existential invertebility – Quality of the intraphysical execution of the existential inversion.

Existential inverter – One who has resolved to execute the existential inversion in intraphysical life.

Existential maximoratorium – Condition of a greater existential moratorium which is given to a completist. It comes as an addition to his or her finished existential program; execution of a healthy extension to an existential mandate that has been concluded.

Existential maxiprogram – Maximal existential program having a wholesale approach. It targets the execution of tasks of universalism and maxifraternity having polykarmic bases.

Existential minimoratorium – Condition of a lesser existential moratorium which is given to an incompletist intraphysical consciousness. It comes as an opportunity to compensate for their holokarmic deficit or to achieve the status of completist regarding their existential program; the finishing of a still incomplete existential mandate.

Existential miniprogram – Existential program targeting the execution of a minimal, groupkarmic task.

Existential moratorium – An extension of the intraphysical life given to selected intraphysical consciousnesses according to their holokarmic merit. An existential moratorium can be based either on a performance deficit (existential minimoratorium) or on a performance surplus (existential maximoratorium) of the individual's existential program.

Existential moratoriumist – One who receives an existential moratorium.

Existential multicompletism – Existential completism obtained through the completion of various existential programs in several consecutive intraphysical lives.

Existential program – Specific program, agenda, or plan of each intraphysical consciousness, to be executed in their current intraphysical life.

Existential recyclability – Quality of the intraphysical execution of existential recycling.

Existential recycler – Intraphysical consciousness who resolves to execute the existential recycling.

Existential recycling – Technique for the realization of one's existential program, executed by a human consciousness, based on changing the perspective and reprioritizing one's life.

Existential robotization – Condition of a tropospheric intraphysical consciousness who is enslaved to intraphysicality or quadridimensionality.

Existential self-mimicry – Imitation of one's own past experiences, be they related to their present intraphysical life or to previous intraphysical lives.

Existential seriality – 1. Evolutionary existential seriality of the consciousness; successive existences; intraphysical rebirths in series. 2. Intraphysical or human life. Outworn synonym: reincarnation; this archaic word no longer serves those more serious individuals dedicated to leading-edge consciousness research.

Extraphysical – Relative to what is outside, or beyond, the intraphysical or human state; consciential state less physical than the human body; non-physical. Outworn synonym: astral.

Extraphysical agenda – Written list of high priority extraphysical, consciential targets – beings, places or ideas – that the projected individual seeks to gradually reach, in a chronological manner, by establishing intelligent plans for his or her development.

Extraphysical approach – Contact of a consciousness with another in extraphysical dimensions.

Extraphysical assistantial facility – Extraphysical treatment center of an intraphysical epicenter (penta practitioner); extraphysical assistantial center or clinic. The resources and extraphysical installations of the extraphysical assistantial facility are numerous and remarkable. The extraphysical assistantial facility is a domiciliary holothosene. (The term "ofiex" is used as a neologism of the Portuguese language).

Extraphysical catatonia – Fixed condition whereby a projected intraphysical consciousnesses perform stereotypical repetitive acts that are generally useless or dispensable in terms of their evolution.

Extraphysical community – A common lifestyle setting of extraphysical consciousnesses in an extraphysical dimension.

Extraphysical consciousness – Paracitizen of extraphysical society; disembodied consciousness. Outworn synonyms: discarnate.

Extraphysical euphoria – Euphoria experienced after biological death due to the reasonably satisfactory completion of one's existential program; postmortem euphoria; paraeuphoria; postsomatic euphoria.

Extraphysical melancholy – Condition of extraphysical, postsomatic or postmortem melancholy, usually generated by a condition of incompletism; paramelancholy.

Extraphysical monitoring – Condition wherein assistance is given by healthy extraphysical consciousnesses to a balanced intraphysical consciousness, while performing balanced tasks of consolation or clarification.

Extraphysical plunder – Action of a group of energyvorous extraphysical consciousnesses, including extraphysical blind guides, in paratropospheric (crustal) dimensions for the purpose of vampirizing intraphysical consciousnesses. It usually happens in surroundings of celebrations or during intraphysical events which gather persons prone to collective intrusive victimization through consciential energies.

Extraphysical precognition (*Latin: pre, before; cognoscere, know*) – Perceptive faculty whereby a consciousness, while fully projected outside the human body, becomes aware of unknown upcoming facts, as well as objects, scenes and distant forms, in the future.

Extraphysical romance – Totality of acts whereby an intraphysical consciousness maintains a healthy or positive romantic relationship while projected outside the body.

Extraphysical society – Society of extraphysical consciousnesses. Population of the extraphysical dimensions.

Free consciousness (*Latin: con + scientia, with knowing*) – Extraphysical consciousness who has definitively liberated themselves (deactivation) from the psychosoma or emotional body and the web of existential seriality (rebirth cycle). A free consciousness is situated in the evolutionary hierarchy above the *Homo sapiens serenissimus.*

Geoenergy (*geo + energy*) – Immanent energy deriving from the soil or earth and absorbed by an intraphysical consciousness through the prekundalini (sole) chakras. Outworn expression: telluric energy.

Golden cord – Supposed energetic element – similar to a remote control – that maintains the mentalsoma connected to the extraphysical brain of the psychosoma.

Graphothosene (*grapho + tho + sen + ene*) – The thosenic signature of a human consciousness.

Group of existential inverters – Intraphysical consciousnesses meeting together in groups, objectifying experimentation in planned existential inversion.

Group of existential recyclers – Intraphysical consciousnesses meeting together in groups, objectifying experimentation in planned existential recycling.

Groupality – Quality of the evolutionary group of a consciousness; condition of group evolutionality.

Groupkarma (*group + karma*) – Principle of cause and effect acting in the evolution of the consciousness, when pertaining to the evolutionary group. State wherein one's free will is bound to one's evolutionary group.

Groupkarmic course – Sum total of stages (phases) that a consciousness undergoes within the scope of one's evolutionary consciential group.

Groupkarmic interprison – Condition wherein a consciousness suffers from groupkarmic inseparability.

Groupthosene – A sectarian, corporate, antipolykarmic thosene. A groupthosene can also be constructive.

Gynochakra (*gyno + chakra*) – Sexchakra of a woman.

Gynosoma (*gyno + soma*) – The female human body, specialized in the animal reproduction of the intraphysical life of the consciousness; aphrodisiac body.

Gynothosene (*gyno + tho + sen + ene*) – Specific thosene of the feminine language and communicability.

Hallucination (*Latin: hallucinari, to err*) – Apparent perception of an external object that is not present in the moment; mental error in one's sensory perceptions which are not founded in objective reality.

Helper – Extraphysical consciousness who assists or serves as an auxiliary to one or more intraphysical consciousnesses; extraphysical benefactor. Outworn expressions: mentor; spirit guide.

Heterothosene (*hetero + tho + sen + ene*) – The thosene of another in relation to ourself.

Holoarchive – Compilation of information from artifacts of knowledge.

Holochakra (*holo + chakra*) – Extraphysical energetic body of the human consciousness. Sum total of all chakras in one's energetic system; energetic double; energetic body; pranic body.

Holochakral existence – Intraphysical life or the existential seriality of the intraphysical existences of human consciousnesses.

Holochakral intrusion – Invasion of an intraphysical consciousness by another using the holochakra or consciential energies; energetic intrusion.

Holochakral looseness – Condition of relative freedom of action of the energetic parabody of an intraphysical consciousness, as compared to their psychosoma and soma.

Holochakral seduction – Energetic action of one consciousness over another (or others) with a more-or-less conscious intention of domination.

Holochakrality – Quality of the manifestations of intraphysical consciousnesses deriving from the holochakra.

Holokarma (*holo + karma*) – The 3 types of consciential actions and reactions – egokarma, groupkarma and polykarma – within the acting principles of cause and effect in the evolution of the consciousness. Egokarma, groupkarma and polykarma when considered together as a whole.

Holomaturity (*holo + maturity*) – Condition of integrated maturity – biological, psychological, holosomatic and multidimensional – of the human consciousness.

Holomemory (*holo + memory*) – Causal, compound, multimillenary, multiexistential, implacable, uninterrupted, personal memory that retains all facts relative to the consciousness; multimemory; polymemory.

Holorgasm (*holo + orgasm*) – Holosomatic orgasm; maximum ecstasy generated through the energy of the entire holosoma.

Holosoma (*holo + soma*) – Set of vehicles of manifestation (bodies) of the intraphysical consciousness: soma, holochakra, psychosoma and mentalsoma; set of vehicles of manifestation of the extraphysical consciousness: psychosoma and mentalsoma.

Holosomatic homeostasis – Integrated, healthy state of harmony of the holosoma.

Holosomatic interfusion – State of maximal sympathetic assimilation between 2 consciousnesses.

Holosomatic intrusion – Invasion of an intraphysical consciousness by another using the entire holosoma.

Holothosene (*holo* + *tho* + *sen* + *ene*) – Aggregated or consolidated thosenes. Defines the characteristics of environments, ideas, objects, or people. This word generates resistance in a wide band of serious readers of the sciences.

Homo sapiens serenissimus – A consciousness who is integrally experiencing the condition of lucid serenism; a consciousness who is about to pass through the third desoma (end of rebirth cycle). Popular synonym: Serenissimus.

Homothosene (*homo* + *tho* + *sen* + *ene*) – Thosene related to telepathic emission and reception; according to conscientiometry, unit of measurement in telepathy.

Hyperacuity – The quality of maximum lucidity of an intraphysical consciousness, achieved through the – greatest possible – recuperation of their cons.

Hyperthosene (*hyper* + *tho* + *sen* + *ene*) – Heuristic thosene; original idea of a discovery; neophilic thosene; unit of measurement of invention, according to conscientiology.

Hypnagogy (*Greek: hipnos, sleep; and agogos, conductor*) – Transitional twilight condition of the consciousness between the waking state and natural sleep. It is an altered state of consciousness.

Hypnopompy (*Greek: hipnos, sleep; and pompikós, procession*) – A transitional condition of natural sleep, prior to physical awakening. It is a semi-asleep state that precedes the act of waking up. It is characterized by dream images having auditory effects and hallucinatory visions that may continue even after waking. It is an altered state of consciousness.

Hypothosene (*hypo* + *tho* + *sen* + *ene*) – Same as protothosene or phytothosene.

Immanent energy – Primary energy, totally impersonal, neutral and dispersed in all objects or realities in the universe, in an omnipotent fashion. Immanent energy has not been tamed by any human consciousness. It is too subtle to be detected by existing instruments.

Incomplete couple – Couple composed of a man and woman who do not form an intimate couple (a couple who has complete sexual interactions), but who, nevertheless, maintain strong affectionate ties.

Incompletism – See existential incompletism.

Integrated maturity – State of a more evolved consciential maturity beyond biological (physical) or mental (psychological) maturity; holomaturity.

Interassistantial – Of or pertaining to mutual assistance.

Interassistantiality – The evolutionary necessity for human consciousnesses to assist each other through logical, just, and mature interassistantial tasks.

Intersciential climate – Condition of multi-understanding in an interconsciential encounter, established through affined thosenes, especially those charged with consciential energy. Interconsciential climates can vary greatly in intensity.

Interconsciential intrusion – Intrusive or invasive action exercised by a consciousness upon another.

Interdimensionality – Interaction, interrelation or interconsciential communication between intraphysical and extraphysical dimensions.

Intermissibility – Quality of the period of intermission between two intraphysical lives of a consciousness.

Intermission – The extraphysical period between two physical lives of a consciousness (existantial seriality). The expression "intermissive period" is a synonym of intermission.

Intermissive course – Sum total of disciplines as well as theoretical and practical experiences administered to extraphysical consciousnesses during their period of consciential intermission between two intraphysical lives. This course occurs when one has achieved a reasonable evolutionary level in one's cycle of personal existences. The objective of the intermissive course is consciential completism in the next intraphysical life.

Interpersonal apparition – Appearance of a projector's psychosoma before intraphysical consciousnesses.

Intimate couple – A couple who has sexual interactions, as opposed to an incomplete couple.

Intraconsciential compensation – Conscientiometric technique based on the use of one's maximum consciential attribute or more developed trait (strong trait) to overcome less developed consciential attributes (weak traits) of one's consciential micro-universe.

Intraconsciential recycling – Intraconsciential, existential, intraphysical recycling or the cerebral renovation of an intraphysical consciousness through the creation of new synapses (interneuronal connections). The newly created synapses allow the adjustment of one's existential program, the execution of existential recycling, existential inversion, the acquisition of new ideas, neothosenes, hyperthosenes, and other neophilic conquests of the self-motivated human consciousness.

Intraconscientiality – Quality of the specific intimate manifestations of the consciousness.

Intraphysical consciousness – Human personality; citizen of intraphysical society. Outworn synonym: incarnate.

Intraphysical euphoria – Euphoria experienced before somatic deactivation that is generated through the reasonably satisfactory completion of one's existential program; premortem euphoria. Ideal condition predisposing one to have a positive existential moratorium.

Intraphysical melancholy – Condition of intraphysical or premortem melancholy (usually generated by consciential ectopia).

Intraphysical societal virus – Any social weak trait in the intraphysical life of human consciousnesses.

Intraphysical society – Society of intraphysical consciousnesses; human society.

Intraphysicality – Condition of intraphysical or human life, or of the existence of the human consciousness.

Intrathosene (*intra* + *tho* + *sen* + *ene*) – Intraconsciential thosene of the human consciousness.

Intrudability – Quality of the pathological, interconsciential thosenic intrusion. Many intraphysical consciousnesses are defensive regarding this word. Outworn equivalent expression: obsession.

Intruder – Perturbed, ill, needy, anticosmoethical consciousness, specially an extraphysical consciousness when performing a thosenic intrusion upon an intraphysical consciousness.

Intrusion-freeness – Quality of a permanently-totally-intrusion-free consciousness.

Intrusive stigma – An evolutionary failure or derailing that is always dramatic and generally pathological, usually stemming from consciential self-intrusion. This process generates either intraphysical or extraphysical melancholy and often results in parapsychic accidents.

Locked existence – Human experience or existential seriality without the production of conscious projections; tropospheric human life having only unconscious, vegetative projections characteristic of the state of evolutionary paracoma; locked existential seriality.

Lucid projectability – Lucid, projective paraphysiological quality of consciousnesses capable of provoking the non-alignment of their holosoma, through willpower, as well as by other means.

Lucidity-recall binomial – Set of two conditions indispensable to the intraphysical consciousness for the achievement of a fully satisfactory lucid projection outside the human body.

Macrosoma (*macro + soma*) – Soma that is supercustomized for the execution of a specific existential program.

Materthosene (*mater + tho + sen + ene*) – Mother-idea or matrix to the complete development of a thesis, theory or essay; leitmotif; major pillar or thosene predominant in a holothosene.

Maxifraternity – Most evolved, universalistic, interconsciential condition that is based on pure fraternity on the part of a self-unrelenting yet heteroforgiving consciousness who forgives others for transgressions but not themselves; megabrotherhood. Maxifraternity is an inevitable goal in the evolution of all consciousnesses. Synonym: Megafraternity.

Maxithosene (*maxi + tho + sen + ene*) – Thosene peculiar to the Free Consciousnesses.

Megagoal – A greater evolutionary objective for a consciousness.

Megapower – The evolved condition of cosmoethical, maximum consciential lucidity.

Megastrong trait – The maximal strong trait of a consciousness.

Megathosene (*mega + tho + sen + ene*) – Same as Orthothosene.

Megaweak trait – The maximal weak trait of a consciousness.

Mentalsoma (*mental + soma*) – Mental body; discernment parabody of the consciousness.

Mentalsomatic cycle – The evolutionary cycle or course that a consciousness initiates upon the definitive deactivation of the psychosoma (third death), consequently living only with the mentalsoma in the condition of a free consciousness.

Mentalsomaticity – Quality of the manifestations of intraphysical consciousnesses deriving from the mentalsoma.

Metasoma (*meta + soma*) – Same as psychosoma, the extraphysical instrument or body of extraphysical and intraphysical consciousnesses.

Minithosene (*mini + tho + sen + ene*) – Thosene of a child, sometimes as a function of their still developing brain.

Mnemonic intrusion – Collision of the intrusive memory of an extraphysical consciousness upon the cerebral memory of an intraphysical consciousness who has been intruded upon (para-amnesia).

Mnemosoma (*mnemo + soma*) – The soma considered specifically in relation to all forms of memory of the consciousness.

Mnemothosene – Unit of measurement of the memory of the consciousness (mnemosomatics and retrocognitions).

Monothanatose – Same as desoma; first death.

Monothosene (*mono + tho + sen + ene*) – Repetitive thosene; fixed idea; mental echo; rethosene.

Moratoriumist – See existential moratoriumist.

Morphothosene (*morpho + tho + sen + ene*) – A thought or a group of thoughts when gathered together and expressed as having some type of form. An accumulation of morphothosenes composes a holothosene. Outworn expression: thought-form.

Multidimensional self-conscientization – Condition of mature lucidity of an intraphysical consciousness in terms of living a multidimensionally evolved consciential life. This condition is achieved through lucid projectability.

Multi-existential cycle – System or condition of our current, average evolutionary level, in which there is a continuous alternation of an intraphysical rebirth period (existential seriality) and a postsomatic extraphysical period (intermission).

Near-Death Experience (NDE) – Involuntary or forced projection due to critical circumstances involving a human consciousness. The NDE is common in cases of terminal illness and survivors of clinical death.

Neophilia – Easy adaptation by an intraphysical consciousness to new situations, things and occurrences. Opposite of neophobia.

Neophobia – Fear of new situations, things and occurrences. Opposite of neophilia.

Neothosene (*neo + tho + sen + ene*) – Thosene of an intraphysical consciousness when operating with new synapses or interneuronal connections – a situation capable of provoking intraconsciential recycling; unit of measurement of consciential renovation, according to conscientiology or, more appropriately, conscientiometry.

Nosothosene – Unit of measurement of the parapathology of the mentalsoma (mentalsomatics and conscientiotherapy).

Oneirothosene – (*oneiro + tho + sen + ene*) – Dream thosene. Same as pathothosene.

Orgasmic aura (*Latin: aura, wisp of air*) Holochakral energy of *facies sexualis* of a man or woman at the exact moment of sexual orgasm or climax.

Orthothosene (*ortho + tho + sen + ene*) – A just or cosmoethical thosene, pertaining to consciential holomaturity; according to conscientiometry, a unit of measurement of practical cosmoethics.

Pangraphy – Broad, sophisticated multimodal psychic writing.

Para – Prefix that signifies beyond or beside, as in parabrain. Also means extraphysical.

Para-anatomy – Para-anatomy is the anatomy that transcends intraphysicality according to the different vehicles of manifestations of the consciousness other than the soma. It is a subfield of holosomatics.

Parabrain – Extraphysical brain of the psychosoma.

Paragenetics – The integral genetics that encompasses the holosomatic inheritances of the consciousness through the psychosoma and mentalsoma (holosomatics), from the retrosomas of previous lives up to the current human embryo. Paragenetics is a research area of conscientiology.

Paraman – Extraphysical consciousness having the appearance of a man or projected man. Outworn and improper synonymous expression: male spiritual entity.

Parapathology – Pathology of the vehicles of manifestation of the consciousness, excluding the human body or soma. Parapathology is a research area of conscientiology.

Paraphysiology – Physiology of the vehicles of manifestation of the consciousness, excluding the human body or soma.

Parapsychophysical repercussions – Reactions between two vehicles of consciential manifestation when they enter into contact with each other. They can be different vehicles of the same consciousness or similar vehicles of two or more consciousnesses. These repercussions can be intraphysical and extraphysical.

Parasanitarian isolation – Temporary assistantial enclosure and energetic neutralization of the thosenic manifestations of one or more ill consciousnesses (intraphysical and/or extraphysical), especially energetic or intrusive manifestations. It is analogous to the sanitarian isolation existing in hospitals that treat patients with a high level of radioactive or toxic contamination, or with infecta-contagious diseases.

Parasurgery – Surgery performed through parapsychism, which transcends intraphysical resources.

Paratherapeutics – The set of therapeutics and treatments developed by conscientiotherapy for the care of sick consciousnesses.

Parathosene (*para* + *tho* + *sen* + *ene*) – Thosene of an extraphysical consciousness.

Parawoman – Extraphysical consciousness having the appearance of a woman or projected woman. Outworn and improper synonymous expression: female spiritual entity.

Pathothosene (*patho* + *tho* + *sen* + *ene*) – Pathological thosene or a thosene of consciential dementia; peccadillo; sick intention; cerebral rumination.

Penile aura – Sexchakral energy around the penis, notably when in erection, perceivable by any motivated individual, especially by the sexually excited man.

Penta (*pe* + *en* + *ta*) – Multidimensional, daily, personal energetic task which receives continuous assistance from the helpers on a long-term basis or for the rest of life. This technique is performed by an intraphysical consciousness in the waking state with the purpose of assisting ill, needy extraphysical or projected consciousnesses. Popular expression: passes-to-the-dark.

Permanently-totally-intrusion-free consciousness – Intraphysical consciousness who is completely self-aware of his or her condition of being permanently and totally free of intrusion.

Personal experience – Non-transferable, direct, personal experimentation by an intraphysical consciousness who is on his or her evolutionary path.

Personal principles – Package of guiding values and initiatives of consciential life, chosen and manifested day-by-day by a consciousness through holomaturity, multidimensionality and applied cosmoethics.

Phenomenon concomitant to CP – Phenomenon, whether within the time-space continuum or not, occurring simultaneously with a conscious projection, in a spontaneous or unexpected manner.

Physical base – Safe locale, chosen by intraphysical consciousnesses to leave their soma in repose while consciously projected to another, exterior, consciential dimension; dualdrome. A domiciliary projectiogenic holothosene. Has a direct relation to: energetically shielded chamber; penta; consciential epicenter; extraphysical assistantial facility; *projetarium*; precognitarium; retrocognitarium.

Phytothosene (*phyto + tho + sen + ene*) – The rudimentary thosene of a plant; the lexical unit of a plant, according to conscientiology.

Podosoma (*podo + soma*) – The soma when considered specifically in regards to the application of feet or foot-related work, as in the case of a soccer player.

Polykarma (*poly + karma*) – Principle of cause and effect active in the evolution of the consciousness, when centered in an experience of cosmic maxifraternity, beyond egokarma and groupkarma.

Polykarmality – Quality of the polykarmic manifestations of the consciousness.

Postsomatic intermissive period – The extraphysical period of a consciousness immediately following their somatic deactivation.

Precognitarium – Physical base technically prepared for the production of precognitive conscious projections.

Pre-couple – Preliminary stage in human sexuality within intraphysical society; flirting.

Pre-intraphysical mandate – Existential program for human life, planned before the intraphysical rebirth of a consciousness; existential program.

Prekundalini – Secondary chakra at the sole of each foot. There are 2 pre-kundalini chakras in the holosoma of an intraphysical consciousness – one on the bottom of each foot. This is a conscientiological expression.

Preserenissimus – Intraphysical or extraphysical consciousness who does not yet live a life of lucid serenism (see *Homo sapiens serenissimus*).

Presomatic intermissive period – The extraphysical period of a consciousness immediately preceding their intraphysical rebirth.

Primothosene (*primo + tho + sen + ene*) – Same as the First Cause of the universe; the first compound thought. This term has no plural form.

Projectiology (*Latin: projectio, projection; Greek: logos, treatise*) – Projectiology is the area of conscientiology that studies the projections of the consciousness and their effects, including the projections of consciential energies outside of the holosoma. It is a sub-field of communicology.

Projective mental target – Predetermined goal that an intraphysical consciousness endeavors to reach using will, intention, mental focus and decision upon finding themselves lucid while outside the body.

Projective phenomenon – A specific psychic occurrence within the scope of projectiological research.

Projective recess – Existential phase of an intraphysical consciousness characterized by a spontaneous cessation – almost always temporary – within a sequence of intensive lucid projective experiences.

Projetarium – Physical base technically prepared for the production of projections of the consciousness.

Prothosene – Unit of measurement of apologies.

Protothosene (*proto + tho + sen + ene*) – More rudimentary thosene; same as phytothosene or hypothosene.

Psychic (parapsychic) accident – Physical or psychological disturbance generated through energetic, interconsciential or pathological influences, generally having an extraphysical or multidimensional origin.

Psychic (parapsychic) signs – Existence, identification and self-aware employment of energetic, animic, psychic and personal signs that all intraphysical consciousnesses possess.

Psychosoma (*Greek: psyche, soul; soma, body*) – Emotional parabody of the consciousness; non-physical body; the objective body of the projected intraphysical consciousness. Outworn synonymous expression: astral body.

Psychosomatic intrusion – Invasion of a consciousness by another through emotionality, or through the psychosoma.

Rethosene (*re + tho + sen + ene*) – Repeated thosene. Same as monothosene or fixed idea.

Retrocognitarium – Physical base technically prepared for the production of retrocognitive conscious projections.

Retrocognition (*Latin: retro, back; cognoscere, to know*) – Perceptive capacity whereby an intraphysical consciousness knows facts, scenes, forms, objects, successes, and experiences that pertain to a time in the distant past. These issues commonly have to do with their holomemory.

Retrothosene (*retro* + *tho* + *sen* + *ene*) – Thosene specifically related to self-retrocognitions; same as the engram of mnemotechnics; the unit of measurement of retrocognitions, according to conscientiometry.

Self-conscientiality – Quality of the level of self-knowledge of a consciousness; megaknowledge.

Self-mimicricity – Consciential quality of the existential self-mimicry.

Self-projection – The intentional or willful departure of the intraphysical consciousness to another consciential dimension, utilizing the psychosoma or the mentalsoma.

Self-relay – Advanced condition in which a more lucid consciousness evolves by consecutively interweaving various intraphysical existences together.

Self-thosene (*self* + *tho* + *sen* + *ene*) – Thosene of the consciousness itself.

Self-unforgiving – Intraphysical consciousnesses who does not pardon their own errors or omissions, in order to eliminate conscious self-corruption. This positive state supports the likewise healthy condition of heteroforgiver, a sincere universal forgiver of all beings, forever – a basic principle of megabrotherhood.

Semi-conscious projection (SCP) – Dreamlike experience in which a projected intraphysical consciousness finds him or herself lucid to some degree, in a confused manner; lucid dream. It is not an ideal projection of the consciousness.

Sene (*sen* + *ene*) – Sentiment and consciential energy.

Serenissimus – Popular name for *Homo sapiens serenissimus.*

Seriality – Quality of the consciousness submitted to existential seriality (rebirth cycle).

Sexchakra (*sex* + *chakra*) – Root or sexual chakra of the human consciousness. Ancient expression related to the consciential energy of this chakra: kundalini (serpentine fire).

Sexsoma (*sex* + *soma*) – The soma when considered specifically in relation to its sex.

Sexthosene (*sex* + *tho* + *sen* + *ene*) – Sexual fantasy; the unit of measurement of mental adultery, according to conscientiometry.

Shielded chamber – Energetically defended and extraphysically "aseptic" private room in a house or apartment, especially a bedroom; intrusion-proof bedroom.

Silver cord – Energetic connection between the soma and the psychosoma present in a projection of the consciousness, resulting from the holochakral energies.

Soma (*Greek: soma, body*) – Human body; physical body. Body of an individual in the Animal kingdom, *Chordata* phylum, *Mammiferous* class, *Primates* order, *Hominidae* family, *Homo* genus, and *Homo sapiens* species, which is the most elevated level of animal on this planet, nonetheless, this is the most rudimentary body or vehicle of the holosoma of the human consciousness.

Spermatic intrusion – Introduction of a man's sperm into a woman's sexsoma during the sex act.

Standard-conduct – Typical pattern of behavior.

Strong trait – Strong point or trait of the personality of an intraphysical consciousness; positive component of the structure of one's consciential micro-universe that propels the evolution of the consciousness.

Subthosene (*sub* + *tho* + *sen* + *ene*) – Thosene charged with consciential energy from the abdominal sub-brain, most notably energy of the umbilicalchakra; the unit of measurement of the abdominal sub-brain, according to conscientiometry.

Suspended animation – That state in which an intraphysical consciousness has temporarily suspended the vital functions of their cellular body, later returning to normal physiological conditions. In certain cases, this occurs without suffering any damage to personal health – the cells survive in a metabolism of human hibernation.

Sympathetic assimilation – Willful assimilation (absorption) of the consciential energies of another consciousness. This condition is often accompanied by the decoding of a set of thosenes of another consciousness. (The term "assim" is used as a neologism of the Portuguese language).

Sympathetic de-assimilation – Cessation of the sympathetic assimilation of consciential energies through the use of one's will, normally by installing the vibrational state. (The term "desassim" is used as a neologism of the Portuguese language).

Tachythosene (*tachy + tho + sen + ene*) – Rapid thosene, natural to the intraphysical consciousness with tachypsychism (quick thinking).

Telethosene (*tele + tho + sen + ene*) – Same as homothosene.

Theorice (*theor + ice*) – Experience of both theory and practice on the part of an intraphysical or extraphysical consciousness.

Thosen (*tho + sen*) – Thought and sentiment.

Thosene (*tho + sen + ene*) – Practical unit of manifestation of the consciousness, according to conscientiology, that considers thought or idea (conception), sentiment or emotion, and consciential energy as being 3 inseparable elements.

Thosener – Instrument through which the consciousness manifests their thoughts and acts. In the case of intraphysical consciousness, the fundamental thosener is the soma.

Thosenic intrusion – Invasion of a consciousness upon another by way of the mentalsoma.

Thosenity – Quality of one's thosenic awareness.

Trithanatose – Deactivation and discarding of the psychosoma, causing a *Homo sapiens serenissimus* to reach the condition of Free Consciousness; third death; third desoma.

Umbilicalchakra (*umbilical + chakra*) – Chakra located above the navel. Related to the (abdominal) physiology and paraphysiology of the human consciousness.

Universalism – Set of ideas derived from the universality of the basic laws of nature and the universe. Universalism inevitably becomes the dominant philosophy of the consciousness, as a result of our natural evolution; cosmism.

Vehicle of the consciousness – Instrument or body whereby the consciousness manifests in intraphysicality (in the case of an intraphysical consciousness) and in the extraphysical dimensions (in the case of a projected individual and an extraphysical consciousness).

Verbaction (*verb + action*) – Coherent interaction between what is said and done by a consciousness; result of one's words being ratified by one's actions.

Vibrational state – Technical condition of maximal dynamization of the holochakral energies, through the impulse of will.

Waking non-alignment – Parapsychic condition in which the intraphysical projector, while in the ordinary waking state, perceives that the psychosoma is in non-alignment or not completely integrated with the soma. This generates the intensification of psychic perceptions and energetic and psychic phenomena.

Weak trait – Weak point or trait of the personality of an intraphysical consciousness; negative component of the structure of one's consciential micro-universe that the individual is not yet able to overcome.

Willful intrusion – Invasion of the will of a consciousness by another through heterosuggestion or heterohypnosis.

Xenophrenia (*Greek: xenos, strange; phrem, mind*) – State of human consciousness outside the normal pattern of waking state, induced by physical, physiological, psychological, pharmacological or parapsychic agents; altered state of consciousness.

Xenothosene (*xeno + tho + sen + ene*) – Meddlesome thosene of an intruder in the occurrences of thosenic intrusion; mental wedge; unit of measurement of interconsciential intrusion, according to conscientiometry.

Zoothosene (*zoo + tho + sen + ene*) – Thosene of an unaware sub-human animal; unit of measurement of a sub-human animal's consciential principle, according to conscientiometry.

CONSCIENTIOLOGY
RESEARCH AREAS

The following are the 70 research areas or scientific specialties, within the ample universe of research in conscientiology and its major scientific fields:

1. Androsomatics. Androsomatics is the area of conscientiology that specifically studies the male soma or androsoma and its relations with the human consciousness (intraphysical consciousness). It is a field of sexsomatics.

2. Assistantiology. Assistantiology is the area of conscientiology that studies the techniques of interconsciential assistance, especially with regards to their effects on the consciousness as a "whole", that is, holosomatic, multimillenary and seeking holomaturity. It is a task of lucid solidarity among consciousnesses leading to megabrotherhood. It is a field of conviviology.

3. Communicology. Communicology is the area of conscientiology that studies all forms of communication of the consciousness, including the interconsciential communication between consciential dimensions. Communicology takes into account the lucid projectability and the consciousness considered as a "whole". It is a field of experimentology.

4. Compucommunicology. Compucommunicology is the area of conscientiology that studies applied computer sciences in communicative and didactic contexts of the consciousness considered as a "whole". It is a field of parapedagogy.

5. Conscientiocentrology. Conscientiocentrology is the area of conscientiology that studies the social philosophy which focuses its objectives on the consciousness per se and in the evolution of the consciousness. It does so through the establishment and maintenance of a *conscientiocentric institution* in the conscientiological intraphysical society, which functions like a consciential cooperative and is based on both the employment and consciential bonds. It is a field of parasociology.

6. Conscientiometry. Conscientiometry is the area of conscientiology that studies conscientiological measurements by applying instruments and methods offered by conscientiology. These resources are capable of establishing the possible bases for the *mathematical analysis of the consciousness*. For example, the conscientiogram is an instrument used by conscientiometry. It is a field of holomaturology.

7. Conscientiotherapy. Conscientiotherapy is the area of conscientiology that studies the treatment, alleviation and remission of disturbances of the consciousness by applying resources and techniques offered by conscientiology according to the pathologies and parapathologies of the consciousness. It is a field of experimentology.

8. Conviviology. Conviviology is the area of conscientiology that studies the consciential communicability with respect to the interrelationships established between consciousnesses who co-exist in any dimension as well as the evolutionary, holokarmic consequences of these relationships. It is a field of communicology.

9. Cosmoanalysis. Cosmoanalysis is the area of conscientiology that studies the practical application of the *cosmogram* to evaluate the Universe's realities filtered by the multidimensional principles of conscientiology. This is accomplished through a maximal association of ideas (global view), based on the facts (phenomenology) which reach and involve the holothosene of the human personality who is both self and heterocritical. It is a field of communicology.

10. Cosmoconscientiology. Cosmoconscientiology is the area of conscientiology that studies the expansion of consciousness or the cosmoconsciousness phenomenon through the mentalsoma. It is a field of paraperceptiology.

11. Cosmoethics. Cosmoethics is the area of conscientiology that studies the ethics or reflection over the multidimensional, cosmic moral that defines consciential holomaturity. Cosmoethics goes beyond social, intraphysical morals or the morals, which present themselves under any human labels. Cosmoethics is maximal, moral and emotional discernment, it rises from the intimacy of the consciential micro-universe. It is a field of evolutionology.

12. Desomatics. Desomatics is the area of conscientiology that studies the physical, consciential, psychological, social, medicolegal and multidimensional contexts associated with the deactivation of the soma (first death) as well as the second and third desomas and their consequences. It is a field of intraphysicology.

13. Despertology. Despertology is the area of conscientiology that studies the intrusion-free condition or the evolutionary, consciential quality of the intrusion-free consciousness who no longer suffers from pathological interconsciential intrusions and their harmful evolutionary consequences. It is a field of conscientiometry (holomaturology).

14. Egokarmalogy. Egokarmalogy is the area of conscientiology that studies the principles of cause and effect active in the evolution of the consciousness regarding the ego per se. It is a field of holokarmalogy.

15. Evolutionology. Evolutionology is the area of conscientiology that studies the evolution of the consciousness considered in an integral, holosomatic, multiexistential and multidimensional fashion. It is the subject matter specific to evolutionologists or evolutionary orientors. It is a field of thosenology.

16. Experimentology. Experimentology is the area of conscientiology that studies all forms and categories of evolutionary experiments of the consciousness. It is a field of evolutionology.

17. Extraphysicology. Extraphysicology is the area of conscientiology that studies the relations and experiences of the intraphysical consciousness in dimensions other than the intraphysical. It is a field of holoresomatics.

18. Groupkarmalogy. Groupkarmalogy is the area of conscientiology that studies the principles of cause and effect active in the evolution of the consciousness regarding the evolutionary group. It is a field of holokarmalogy.

19. Gynosomatics. Gynosomatics is the area of conscientiology that studies specifically the female soma or gynosoma and its relations with the human consciousness (intraphysical consciousness). It is a field of sexsomatics.

20. Holochakralogy. Holochakralogy is the area of conscientiology that studies the quality of the manifestations of the intraphysical consciousness according to the holochakra or energetic parabody. It is a field of holosomatics.

21. Holokarmalogy. Holokarmalogy is the area of conscientiology that studies the holokarmic account of the consciousness in evolution encompassing egokarmality, groupkarmality and polykarmality. It is a field of evolutionology.

22. Holomaturology. Holomaturology is the area of conscientiology that studies the holomaturity of the human consciousness in all its manifestations and evolutionary consequences. Holomaturity, also known as integral or holosomatic maturity, pertains specifically to the biological, psychological, mental and multidimensional maturity. It is a field of evolutionology.

23. Holoresomatics. Holoresomatics is the area of conscientiology that studies the existential seriality and the evolutionary multiexistential cycles (successive intraphysical resomas) as well as the their implications and repercussions on the human consciousness including the interplanetary migrations. It is a field of experimentology.

24. Holosomatics. Holosomatics is the area of conscientiology that studies the holosoma or the set of vehicles of manifestation of the consciousness, as well as, their functions and applications by the intraphysical or extraphysical consciousness. It is a field of thosenology.

25. Homeostatics. Homeostatics is the area of conscientiology that studies the theorice of *holosomatic homeostasis* or the integral, healthy and harmonious state of the holosoma which allows intraphysical consciousnesses to live better and more efficiently execute their existential programs. It is a field of holosomatics.

26. Intermissiology. Intermissiology is the area of conscientiology that studies the intermissive period of the consciousness in evolution situated between two intraphysical lifetimes within the evolutionary multiexistential cycle. It is a field of extraphysicology.

27. Intraphysicology. Intraphysicology is the area of conscientiology that studies the relations and experiences of the intraphysical consciousness in the intraphysical or human dimension. It is a field of holoresomatics.

28. Invexology. Invexology is the area of conscientiology that studies the philosophical, technical and practical aspects of the human, existential inversion. It is a field of intraphysicology.

29. Macrosomatics. Macrosomatics is the area of conscientiology that studies the macrosoma, the extraordinary soma best suited to the execution of a specific existential program. It is a field of somatics.

30. Mentalsomatics. Mentalsomatics is the area of conscientiology that studies the mentalsoma, the parabody of discernment and its evolutionary consequences to the consciousness. It is a field of holosomatics.

31. Mnemosomatics. Mnemosomatics is the area of conscientiology that studies the soma specifically in relation to the intrasomatic memories starting with the cerebral memory until reaching the holomemory. It is a field of mentalsomatics.

32. Para-anatomy. Para-anatomy is the area of conscientiology that studies the anatomy that transcends intraphysicality according to the different vehicles of manifestations of the consciousness other than the soma. It is a field of holosomatics.

33. Para-anesthesiology. Para-anesthesiology is the area of conscientiology that studies the anesthesia through parapsychism which transcends intraphysical resources. It is a field of parasurgery (conscientiotherapy).

34. Para-asepsis. Para-asepsis is the area of conscientiology that studies the asepsis through parapsychism that transcends intraphysical resources. It is a field of parasurgery (conscientiotherapy).

35. Parabiology. Parabiology is the area of conscientiology that studies living beings and their multidimensional and multivehicular relations. It is a field of experimentology.

36. Parabotany. Parabotany is the area of conscientiology that studies the manifestation of the consciential principles in the primary condition of plants or the paraflora. It is a field of parabiology.

37. Parachronology. Parachronology is the area of conscientiology that studies the chronology of manifestations of consciousnesses that transcends intraphysicality, aiming at the other consciential dimensions, holobiographies and multidimensionality. It is a field of holoresomatics.

38. Paraclinics. Paraclinics is the area of conscientiology that studies the care of sick patients through parapsychism that transcends intraphysical resources. It is a field of conscientiotherapy.

39. Paragenetics. Paragenetics is the area of conscientiology that studies the integral genetics that encompasses the holosomatic inheritances of the consciousness through the psychosoma and mentalsoma. These inheritances come from the retrosomas of previous lives as intraphysical consciousnesses. It is a field of psychosomatics.

40. Parageography. Parageography is the area of conscientiology that studies the description of the paratroposphere, including its extraphysical parageographic landscapes and environments, as well as the relations between these environments and the parapopulation (indigenous and/or transient). It is a field of extraphysicology.

41. Parahealing. Parahealing is the area of conscientiology that studies the healing through parapsychism that transcends intraphysical resources. It is a field of parasurgery.

42. Parahemostasis. Parahemostasis is the area of conscientiology that studies the hemostasis through parapsychism that transcends intraphysical resources. It is a field of parasurgery (conscientiotherapy).

43. Parahistory. Parahistory is the area of conscientiology that studies the history of the consciousness and of the cosmos in a multidimensional fashion through extraphysicology, retrocognitions and lucid projectability. It transcends both the autobiography of the intraphysical consciousness in the current human life, and human history. It is a field of parachronology.

44. Paraneurology. Paraneurology is the area of conscientiology that studies the parabrain and its relations to the physical brain, the nervous system and the other vehicles of the holosoma. It is a field of psychosomatics.

45. Parapathology. Parapathology is the area of conscientiology that studies the pathology of the vehicles of manifestation of the consciousness or the holosoma (holochakra, psychosoma, mentalsoma) excluding the human body (soma). It is a field of holosomatics.

46. Parapedagogy. Parapedagogy is the area of conscientiology that studies the philosophy of education and the pedagogy that transcends the resources of intraphysicality. The study is performed through the lucid multidimensionality and the projectability of the human consciousness and their consequences in human life. It is a field of communicology.

47. **Paraperceptiology.** Paraperceptiology is the area of conscientiology that studies the paraperceptions of the consciousness that transcend the perceptions related to the human body (soma), their phenomena and evolutionary consequences. It is a field of paraphenomenology.

48. **Paraphenomenology.** Paraphenomenology is the area of conscientiology that studies the parapsychic manifestations of the human consciousness whether they have a subjective origin (intraconsciential), an objective origin (perceptible to the external world) or both. It does so through the application of the holosoma and the mobilization of consciential energies. It is a field of paraphysiology.

49. **Paraphysiology.** Paraphysiology is the area of conscientiology that studies the functions of the vehicles of manifestation of the consciousness or holosoma (holochakra, psychosoma and mentalsoma), excluding the human body. It is a field of holosomatics.

50. **Paraprophylaxis.** Paraprophylaxis is the area of conscientiology that studies the prophylaxis that transcends the limits of intraphysicology in order to prevent the consciousness from making mistakes and suffering inconveniences in all the dimensions where it manifests. It is a field of paraclinics (conscientiotherapy).

51. **Pararegeneration.** Pararegeneration is the area of conscientiology that studies the anatomic and/or functional regeneration of the vehicles of manifestation of the consciousness or holosoma, besides the human body. This includes parahealing and paratransfigurations. It is a field of paraphysiology.

52. **Parasemiology.** Parasemiology is the area of conscientiology that studies the investigation and identification of the parasymptomatology and the parasigns of disturbances and parapathologies of the consciousness considered as a "whole" that transcends the intraphysicality. The study is performed through parapsychism and paraperceptiology. It is a field of paraclinics.

53. **Parasociology.** Parasociology is the area of conscientiology that studies the philosophy, techniques and practices of the conscientiological intraphysical society as well as of extraphysical societies and their consequences on human, extraphysical and projective life. It is a field of holoresomatics.

54. **Parasurgery.** Parasurgery is the area of conscientiology that studies the surgery through parapsychism that transcends intraphysical resources (paraperceptiology). It is a field of conscientiotherapy.

55. **Paratechnology.** Paratechnology is the area of conscientiology that studies the technology of the consciousness and its consequences, by applying specific methodologies in order to expand the self-knowledge of the intraphysical consciousness. Here are included the projective techniques. It is a field of extraphysicology.

56. **Paratherapeutics.** Paratherapeutics is the area of conscientiology that studies the therapeutics and treatments developed by conscientiotherapy for the care of sick consciousnesses. It is a field of paraclinics (conscientiotherapy).

57. **Parazoology.** Parazoology is the area of conscientiology that studies the manifestation of the consciential principles in the condition of subhuman animals or the parafauna. It is a field of parabiology.

58. **Polykarmalogy.** Polykarmalogy is the area of conscientiology that studies the principles of cause and effect active in the evolution of the consciousness with regards to the theory and application of cosmic maxifraternity, beyond egokarma and groupkarma. It is a field of holokarmalogy.

59. **Proexology.** Proexology is the area of conscientiology that studies the existential program of intraphysical consciousnesses and its evolutionary consequences. It is a field of intraphysicology.

60. **Projectiocritics.** Projectiocritics is the area of conscientiology that studies the projectiological critique in general, extremely important within the consciential paradigm. It is a field of projectiology.

61. **Projectiography.** Projectiography is the area of conscientiology that performs the technical study of projectiological accounts. It is a field of projectiology.

62. **Projectiology.** Projectiology is the area of conscientiology that studies the projections of the consciousness and their effects, including the projections of consciential energies outside of the holosoma. It is a field of communicology (experimentology).

63. Projectiotherapy. Projectiotherapy is the area of conscientiology that studies the prophylaxis and the therapies derived from the research and techniques of projectiology. It is a field of paraclinics (conscientiotherapy).

64. Psychosomatics. Psychosomatics is the area of conscientiology that studies the emotions of the consciousness, arising from the psychosoma, the parabody of desires. It is a field of holosomatics.

65. Recexology. Recexology is the area of conscientiology that studies the philosophy, technique and practice of existential recycling within intraphysicality, which begins with intraconsciential recycling. It is a field of intraphysicology.

66. Resomatics. Resomatics is the area of conscientiology that studies the somatic rebirth of the extraphysical consciousness who goes into the temporary condition of intraphysical consciousness. In so doing it leaves behind extraphysicality to exist in intraphysicality. It is a field of intraphysicology.

67. Serenology. Serenology is the area of conscientiology that studies the *Homo sapiens serenissimus* (or serenissimus), their personal traits, characteristics and evolutionary consequences. It is a field of conscientiometry (holomaturology).

68. Sexsomatics. Sexsomatics is the area of conscientiology that specifically studies the soma with regards to its sex or the sexsoma and its relations with the intraphysical consciousness whether it is a man or woman. It is a field of somatics.

69. Somatics. Somatics is the area of conscientiology that studies the soma or human body within the holosoma or in relation to the other vehicles of manifestation of the consciousness, in its multidimensional evolution. It is a field of holosomatics.

70. Thosenology. Thosenology is the area of conscientiology that studies the thosenes (*tho*ughts, *sen*timents, *en*ergies), thosenity and the thosenators of the consciousness, their paraphysiology and parapathology. Self-thosenity is the consciousness' mechanism of incessant expression in all manifestations in any dimension. Consequently, thosenology is the concept (theory) and the substrate (practice) which acts as the foundation of conscientiology. This area of conscientiology has not yet (1999) been discovered by conventional science.

INDEX

A

Abdominal sub-brain 121
Absolute certainties 102
Accomplishments
  personal 97, 103
Achievements 100
Acquisition of knowledge 39
Adolescence 43, *50*
Adolescents 43
Admiration-disagreement
    binomial 121
Advanced existential program 121
Agenda 108
  extraphysical 108, *132*
  of the projected projector 108
Altered state of consciousness 121
Alternating intraphysical
    preserenissimus 121
Amentia
  consciential 123
Amorality 64
Androchakra 121
Androsoma 122
Androsomatics 150
Androthosene 122
Animism 122
Anthropology 40
Antithosene 122
Aphrodisiac female sexsoma 122
Appendage
  caudal *33*, 42
Approach
  extraphysical 93, *132*
Arms 72
Artifacts of knowledge 122
Aspirations
  evolutionary 73
Assistantiality 122
Assistantiology 150

Assisted conscious projection 122
Auric coupling 122

B

Basement
  consciential 40, 43, *123*
Basic sexual instinct 44
Belly-brain 58, 122
Biothosene 122
Bithanatose 122
Blind guides
  extraphysical 100, *122*
Body 12
  bellows 37
  energetic 17
  human 12, *37*
Body of ideas 71
Body-Mind dilemma 78
Bond
  consciential 114, 115, *123*
Boys 40
Bradythosene 123
Brain 37
Brainwashing 10, *98*
Breathing 38
Butterfly seeker 77

C

Cardiochakra 123
Catatonia
  extraphysical 132
Chakra 45, *123*
Childhood *35*, 41
Chimpanzees 33
Chirosoma 123
Citizenship
  extraphysical 77
Clarification task 68, 69, 79, *123*
  cosmoethical 68
Climate
  interconsciential 137

BIBLIOGRAPHY

1. VIEIRA, Waldo; Penta Manual: Personal Energetic Task; 138 pages; 34 chapters.; 5 bibliographic references; glossary with 282 terms; 150 abbreviations; alphabetical; 21 x 14 cm; br.; lst edition; Rio de Janeiro, RJ; Brazil; Instituto Internacional de Projeciologia; 1995.

2. IDEM; Miniglossário da Conscienciologia; 57 pages; 17 x 11 cm; Spiral bound; lst edition; Rio de Janeiro, RJ; Brazil; Instituto Internacional de Projeciologia; 1992; page 54.

3. IDEM; O que é a Conscienciologia; 180 pages; 100 chapters.; 3 bibliographic references.; glossary with 280 terms; alphabetical; 21 x 14 cm; br.; lst edition; Rio de Janeiro, RJ; Brazil; Instituto Internacional de Projeciologia; 1994; pages 30, 72, 107, 139, 156, 160, 168, 173.

4. IDEM; Projeciologia: Panorama das Experiências da Consciência Fora do Corpo Humano; XXVIII + 900 pages; 475 chapters; 40 illustrations; 1.907 bibliographic references; glossary with 15 terms; 58 abbreviations; ono.; geo.; alphabetical; 27 x 18,5 x 5 cm; enc.; 3rd edition; Londrina; Paraná; Brazil; Livraria e Editora Universalista; 1990; pages 389-393.

5. IDEM; Projections of the Consciousness: A Diary of Out-of-Body Experiences: 224 pages; glossary with 25 terms; alphabetical; 21 x 14 cm; br.; 4th edition revised; Rio de Janeiro, RJ; Brazil; Instituto Internacional de Projeciologia; 1992; pages 153-155. (Editions in Portuguese, Spanish and English).

6. IDEM; 700 Experimentos da Conscienciologia; 1058 pages; 700 chapters.; 300 tests; 8 indexes; 2 tabulations; 600 enumerations; ono.; 5.116 bibliographic references; geo.; glossary with 280 terms; alphabetical; 28,5 x 21,5 x 7 cm; enc.; lst edition; Rio de Janeiro, RJ; Brazil; Instituto Internacional de Projeciologia; 1994; pages 171, 178, 180, 183, 198, 242, 283, 322, 352, 353, 355, 409, 412, 424, 431, 432, 468, 484, 539, 542, 564, 572, 580, 595, 671, 672, 693, 700, 726, 736, 737, 739, 741, 759.

INTERNATIONAL INSTITUTE OF PROJECTIOLOGY AND CONSCIENTIOLOGY

The **International Institute of Projectiology and Conscientiology** (IIPC) is a non-profit institution of research and education, or laboratory-school, that has been dedicated to the study of the consciousness (soul, spirit, ego, intelligent principle) and its bioenergetic and projective manifestations (out-of-body experience) since its foundation in 1988. IIPC has been declared a "public federal utility" by the government of Brazil.

Having the objective of disseminating its research findings in conscientiology and Projectiology to researchers and the public, the IIPC has published various books and has developed a regular program of educational activities, conferences, courses, lectures, workshops and other activities at all of its offices. Groups of foreigners regularly visit the Institute, which is able to give its courses in Portuguese, English, Spanish and French.

IIPC STATISTICS (1999)

- 58 Offices including:
  - *Main Office* in Rio de Janeiro.
  - Center of Higher Studies of the Consciousness (CEAEC): in Iguassu Falls, Brazil.
  - 8 *National Offices*: Belo Horizonte, Brasília, Curitiba, Florianópolis, Porto Alegre, Rio de Janeiro, Salvador and São Paulo.
  - 8 *International Offices*: Barcelona, Buenos Aires, Lisbon, London, Madrid, Miami, New York and Ottawa.
- 715 Volunteers.
- 204 Instructors.
- 111 Technical Consultants, specialists in specific subjects.
- 74 *Research Groups* divided into 7 areas: Leading-edge Research Group; Conscientiological Intraphysical Society; Conscientiotherapy; Group of Existential Recyclers; Group of Existential Inverters; Computer Science Group; Indepen-

dent Research. Group and individual research activities began in 1992. All researchers are IIPC volunteers.
- 730 Research Group Participants.
- 99 Researchers.
- Mailing List: A total of 105,860 individuals & institutions; Brazilian mailing list totaling 101,879 (31,500 students) and international mailing list totaling 3,981 (74 countries).
- 43 books and periodicals have been published by IIPC.

Educational Activities. The Technical-Scientific Department, through the Education Center (EDC), coordinates the Institute's educational activities. Education Center is the department that is responsible for the IIPC Teacher Training Program. This program has trained an educational body that, in 1998, was composed of 204 instructors actively teaching IIPC programs in Brazil and abroad.

The EDC operates through a General Coordinating body and its respective divisions. It is based at the IIPC's Main Office in Rio de Janeiro and operates through a Regional Coordination Team that is active in 13 IIPC offices, both in and out of Brazil. A team consisting of 48 Orienting Teachers is responsible for the maintenance and improvement of the Teacher Training Program.

THE IIPC HAS DEVELOPED TWO TYPES OF COURSES:

Regular Courses include those with and without prerequisite. The five stages (in English) are taken in sequence and provide information on the history, ideas and research results achieved over the last 30 years in the field of conscientiology and Projectiology, as well as teaching and allowing practice with various advanced conscientiology and Projectiology techniques.

Extracurricular Courses (ECC) and Special Theme Courses (STC) – Having no prerequisite, these courses are the result of consciential research performed by IIPC teachers in the specializations of conscientiology, projectiology and various fields of study in conventional science.

Lectures - Besides as the courses developed the IIPC, free public lectures are held regularly at all IIPC offices.

PERIODICALS PUBLISHED BY THE IIPC

BIPRO - Boletim de Projeciologia *(Projectiology Bulletin)*,
published by the IIPC Office in Porto Alegre RS, Brazil.

Jornal da Invéxis *(Existential Inversion Newspaper)*,
published by the IIPC Existential Inversion Research Group.

Journal of Conscientiology,
published by the IIPC Office in Miami, USA.

Recéxis *(Existential Recycling)*,
published by the Existential Recycling Research Group.

BOOKS PUBLISHED BY THE IIPC

100 Testes da Conscienciometria
(100 Conscientiometry Tests), Waldo Vieira.

200 Teáticas da Conscienciologia
(200 Conscientiology Theorices), Waldo Vieira.

700 Experimentos da Conscienciologis
(700 Conscientiology Experiments), Waldo Vieira.

A Ciência Conscienciologia e as Ciências Convencionais
(Conscientiology and the Conventional Sciences), Sonia Cerato.

A Natureza Ensina
(Nature Enlightens), Waldo Vieira.

Catálogo de Pesquisas do IIPC
(IIPC Research Catalog), Tânia Ferraro.

Conscienciograma
(Conscientiogram), Waldo Vieira (Portuguese and Spanish).

Despertar para Nova Dimensão
(Awakening to a New Dimension), Francisco de Biaso.

Ensaios Extracorpóreos
(Extracorporeal Teachings), Luiz Araújo.

Evolução em Cadeia
(Evolution in Prison), Claudio Costa.

Gestações Conscienciais I, II & III
(Consciential Gestations I, II & III), Existential Inversion Research Group.

Manual da Dupla Evolutiva
(Evolutionary Duo Manual), Waldo Vieira.

Manual da Proexis
(Existential Program Manual), Waldo Vieira (English and Portuguese).

Manual da Tenepes
(Penta Manual), Waldo Vieira (English, Portuguese and Spanish).

Manual de Redação da Conscienciologia
(Conscientiology Writting Manual), Waldo Vieira.

Máximas da Conscienciologia
(Conscientiology Maxims), Waldo Vieira.

Minidefinições Consciencias
(Consciential Minidefinitions), Waldo Vieira.

Mudar ou Mudar
(To Change or To Change), Flávia Guzzi.

Nossa Evolução
(Our Evolution), Waldo Vieira (English, Portuguese and Spanish).

O Que É a Conscienciologia
(What is Conscientiology), Waldo Vieira

Projeciologia
Panorama das Experiências da Consciência Fora do Corpo Humano
(Projectiology - An Overview of Experiences of the Consciousness Outside of The Human Body), Waldo Vieira.

Projeções da Consciência Diário de Experiências Fora do Corpo Físico
(Projections of the Consciousness Diary of Out of Body Experiences), Waldo Vieira (English, Portuguese and Spanish).

Retrocognições - Lembranças de Vivências Passadas
(Retrocognitions: Recollections of Past Lives), Wagner Alegretti.

Síndrome do Estrangeiro
(The Foreigner Syndrome), Málu Balona.

Temas da Conscienciologia
(Conscientiology Themes), Waldo Vieira.

Vivendo em Múltiplas Dimensões
(Living In Multiple Dimensions), Glória Thiago.

IIPC INTERNATIONAL OFFICES

The IIPC currently has 8 International Offices:

Since 1992, the Buenos Aires, Argentina office has operated as a base serving to integrate conscientiology and projectiology in South American countries, as well as the rest of Latin America.

The New York and Miami offices have been giving activities in English, Spanish and Portuguese since 1994. In this way, they have been addressing the needs of Americans, Brazilian immigrants, Spanish speaking and other interested individuals.

The New York office currently offers the CDP in New York, New Jersey, Connecticut, Massachusetts and California. It maintains contact with various institutions, including the American Society for Psychical Research (ASPR), one of the oldest and most important parapsychology research institutions in the world.

The Miami office, established in 1994, holds its activities in both English and Spanish in Florida and California.

The Ottawa, Canada office holds public lectures and offers IIPC courses on a regular basis since 1996.

In Europe, the IIPC activities are held through its offices in Lisbon, Portugal (since 1994), London, England (since 1995), Barcelona and Madrid, Spain (since 1997).

The IIPC also maintains contact with European researchers, most notably in France, Italy, and Holland.

In Asia, the IIPC is currently holding activities in and around Beijing, China.

IIPC CAMPUS

IIPC Campus is a project that will contribute towards the consolidation of the Consciential Paradigm in intraphysical society through the construction of a multidimensional mega-endeavor in the city of Rio de Janeiro, Brazil.

The implantation of a campus will make various research projects viable, thus guaranteeing the dissemination of the leading-edge ideas of the sciences of conscientiology and Projectiology through educational and research activities, such as courses, books, laboratory experiments, and others.

The Consciential School thus constitutes a priority item in the IIPC Campus Project. Assistantiality that is optimized through education in the form of a Consciential School will be a landmark in terms of the clarification task, whether it be in the development of young projectors, or in the interconsciential work of all those consciousnesses motivated to gain a greater maturity through parapsychic, projective and consciential development.

The construction of buildings for holding extension courses, as well as auditoriums and classrooms for regular IIPC course offerings, will be an integral part of this Complex that will be a catalyzing agent for individual and group advanced existential programs.

Aiming at the deepening of interconsciential and inter-corporate relationships, the IIPC Campus will include spaces for individuals and businesses to work together in the realization of activities of common interest related to education or research.

Individuals can volunteer their time by donating their knowledge, energy and bureaucratic efforts, with a consciential bond, to participate in the areas of administration and publishing, working in workshops and laboratories designed for experimental research aimed at the maintenance of the Institute.

The expansion of the sciences of conscientiology and Projectiology demand continuingly greater interaction between consciousnesses from diverse countries, planets and even dimensions, since evolutionary work is multidimensional in nature. For this reason, hotels and restaurants are planned that will gather people of diverse cultures, languages and nationalities who will come in search of information regarding the leading-edge relative truths of conscientiology.

In this way, the IIPC Campus represents an intercontinental and interdimensional hub aimed at disseminating cutting-edge information in terms of evolutionality, assistantiality, and parapsychic and mentalsomatic development of intraphysical and extraphysical consciousnesses. It will also signify the beginning of a new phase of implantation of various IIPC Campuses around the world.

INVITATION FOR PARTICIPATION

Having the multidimensional and cosmoethical objective of catalyzing the holomaturity of more aware preserenissimus, the IIPC is open to all researchers who are motivated to work with its advanced proposals. If you are interested in working as a *minicog of the maximechanism* of conscientiality, contact the IIPC office nearest you.

IIPC World Headquarters:

Rua Visconde de Pirajá, 572 / 6° andar

Rio de Janeiro, RJ, CEP 22410-002, Brazil

Phone: (021) 512 9229

Fax: (021) 512 4735

E-mail: iipc@iipc.org.br

Home page: http://www.iipc.org.br

Center for Higher Studies of the Consciousness:

C.P. 1027 - Centro - Foz do Iguaçu

PR - CEP 85851-000 - Brazil

Phone/Fax: (045) 525 2652

E-Mail: ceaec@foznet.com.br

Home Page: http://www.ceaec.org

INTERNATIONAL OFFICES

Barcelona:

Calle Consell de Cent, 425/ 3° C

L'Example 08009 Barcelona – Spain

Phone: (3493) 232 8008

Fax: (3493) 232 8010

E-Mail: barcelona@iipc.org

Lisbon:

R. Paschoal de Melo 84 – 1° Esquerdo –

Sala 11

Estefânia 1000 Lisbon – Portugal

Phone/Fax: (351 1) 353 6339

E-Mail: lisboa@iipc.org

Buenos Aires:

Calle Azcuenaga, 797 / 2° A

Capital Federal CP 1029 Buenos Aires –

Argentina

Phone/Fax: (541) 951 5048

E-Mail: buenosaires@iipc.org

London:

45 Great Cumberland Place,

3rd. floor – London W1H 7LH – England

Phone: (44 171) 723 0544

Fax: (44 171) 723 0545

E-Mail: london@iipc.org

Madrid:

Calle Carretas, 12 – 2º /5-6

CP 28012 – Madrid – Spain

Phone: (3491) 701 1375

Fax: (3491) 701 1375

E-Mail: Madrid@iipc.org

New York:

20 East, 49 Street, 2F

New York, 10017, NY – USA

Phone: (1 212) 308 5443

Fax: (1 212) 998 0180

E-Mail: newyork@iipc.org

Miami:

7800 SW 57 Ave., Suite 207 – D

South Miami, Fl 33143 – USA

Phone: (1 305) 668 4668

Fax: (1 305) 668 4663

E-Mail: florida@iipc.org

Ottawa:

Phone: (1 530) 688 9040

Fax: (1 530) 236 6575

E-Mail: ottawa@iipc.org

NATIONAL OFFICES

Belo Horizonte:

Av. Brasil 283, sala 1604 – Santa Efigênia

Belo Horizonte – MG – CEP 30140-000

Phone/Fax: (031) 241 1358

E-Mail: iipcbh@task.com.br

Porto Alegre:

R. Gen. Andrade Neves, 159/ cj. 12

Centro – Porto Alegre – RS- Cep 90010-210

Phone/Fax: (051) 224 0707

E-Mail: iipcpoa@pro.procergs.com.br

Brasília:

SEPS 714/914 SUL – Ed. Porto Alegre

Bl.A – sala 142

Asa Sul – DF – CEP 70390-145

Phone/Fax: (061) 346 5573

E-Mail: iipcbsb@solar.com.br

Salvador:

Centro Empresarial Iguatemi Bloco B

sala 234 – Iguatemi – Salvador – BA –

CEP 41820-020

Phone/Fax: (071) 359 0628

E-Mail: iipcsdr@sunrnp.ufba.br

Curitiba:

R. Visconde de Nácar, 1505 / 9° Andar

Centro Curitiba – PR – CEP 80410-201

Phone/Fax: (041) 233 5736

E-Mail: iipcctb@mps.com.br

São Paulo:

Av. Paulista, 1159 - 3º andar - Bloco 306

São Paulo - SP - CEP 01311-200

Phone/Fax: (011) 287 9705

E-Mail: iipcsp@ibm.net

Florianópolis:

Av. Rio Branco, 354 – sala 810

Centro Florianópolis – SC – CEP 88015-200

Phone: (048) 224 3446 Fax: (048) 346 1530

E-Mail: iipcfln@matrix.com.br

For information on other offices, contact IIPC's headquarters.

CENTER FOR HIGHER STUDIES OF THE CONSCIOUSNESS (CEAEC)

"A center for interaction, research and globalization of
the cutting-edge ideas of conscientiology."

The CEAEC is a proposal for work aimed towards researching the consciousness (ego, personality, self, spirit, soul), that is based on the consciential paradigm. It was founded on June 15, 1995 in the city of Iguassu Falls, in the state of Parana, Brazil.

The CEAEC was structured as a result of the Cooperative of Volunteers' creation of the International Institute of Projectiology and conscientiology Ltd., a cooperative of research and extension. Its creation was based on studies developed through the International Institute of Projectiology and Conscientiology (IIPC), with the objective of creating a conscientiology research center having an ample infrastructure for the development of technical and scientific solutions for catalyzing evolution of the consciousness.

With the realization of this project, the CEAEC has developed an area of 242,996 m², next to the Tamanduazinho river, establishing a hub of research education and dissemination of the ideas of conscientiology.

IGUASSU FALLS

One of the characteristics of Iguassu Falls related to the choice of constructing the CEAEC is the quantity and quality of immanent energy in the location, a fact that helps the holothosene (accumulation of thoughts, sentiments and energies) in the area. Iguassu Falls also stands out due to its strategic location within the Mercosul, or South American Common Market, next to Argentina and Paraguay. It is the second largest touristic area in Brazil, thus receiving a great flow of tourists from around the world. All these aspects of Iguassu Falls contribute towards the globalization of the clarification task.

The CEAEC is open to consciousness researchers, who may or may not wish to be a part of this institution, and exchanges between other related organizations, for the realization of its goal of promoting research. In this way, the research policy of the CEAEC allows access by all those interested in using this infrastructure that favors the experience of the theory and practice of conscientiology in a simple and direct manner, without any intermediaries, through self-research and the realization of personal experiences in its laboratories.

This infrastructure will implant a holothosene that predisposes the consciousness' immersion, thus generating possibilities for clarifying multidimensional experiences that are at the heart of conscientiological research. This allows researchers and scholars to stay as long as they wish at these installations.

Through its research, the CEAEC is facilitating the production of leading-edge ideas. Research is considered the highest level of assistantiality, because it permits the deepening and clarifying of consciousnesses. This undertaking is bringing innumerous benefits of self-knowledge and consciential development, which should expand with the intensification of activities.

Volunteer Cooperative of the International Institute of Projectiology and Conscientiology

The Cooperative of IIPC Volunteers is a cooperative of research and education that was formed in order to build and administrate the CEAEC. The construction of this large consciousness research center is the result of combined efforts of the members of the cooperative, whose bond with the CEAEC is a consciential one (as opposed to an employment bond). Their participation allows the creation of an infrastructure that is directed towards research aiming to amplify the possibilities for performing the clarification task and producing evolution in light of conscientiological ideas.

Administration

The construction and administration of the CEAEC is realized through the efforts of the volunteers who work with a consciential bond, or rather, are linked through the leading-edge ideas of consciential evolution (as opposed to a financial, employment bond). This is realized through the system of cooperativism, as it is the most advanced form of societal organization available and offers a structure that is closest to the ideas of conscientiology.

The financial resources obtained for the administration of the CEAEC come from the quotas paid by the cooperative members, the sale of lots in the conscientiological residential project (being built for future residences based on the principles of the consciential paradigm), books magazines, promotional material and courses. These funds are applied exclusively towards the further construction of the CEAEC, as published monthly in the CEAEC newsletter, sent to all coop members and subscribers.

Experience has shown that, to the degree that the projects of implantation of CEAEC are correctly developed within a multidimensional proposal, the necessary resources appear in the correct amount, and in a manner that is coordinated with the time line of the work.

CEAEC PORTFOLIO

Event Auditorium

The Event Auditorium accommodates 800 persons and hosts diverse events, such as: technical meetings, congresses, symposia, forums, courses, and others. Technical meetings are a highlight, in which brainstorming sessions and debates related to the development of CEAEC projects and conscientiology ideas are held. The CEAEC periodically promotes immersion courses in which the participants are totally immersed in the holothosene of study and research. These constitute opportunities to coalesce ideas on advanced themes in Conscientiology, through presentations, debates and exchanges of experiential knowledge related to consciential research.

These courses involve sessions in the CEAEC consciential laboratories and discussions about these experiments in evaluation meetings. Visits are also occasionally made to touristic locations in Iguassu Falls in order to make observations and evaluate their energetic fields and analyze paraperceptions.

The immersion events also significantly contribute to the increased interaction between the participants, who are housed at the CEAEC "Village" Researcher Housing.

Restaurant /Lounge

Includes reception area, restaurant, industrial and snackbar. This space allows the Center's students and researchers to visit and dine together. This space also serves as an extension of the classrooms, allowing an exchange of multidimensional ideas and experiences, thus becoming another important research laboratory.

Holoarchive

The Holoarchive has an area of 1,500 m². This area is composed of various environments dedicated to the support of consciousness research. It currently includes 52,000 items corresponding to very diverse artifacts of knowledge, and is organized in the following types of archives: books; maps; UFOs; videos; and others, which will be divided into dozens of stands.

These collections will allow the permanent exposition of artifacts of knowledge. The collection of books is among the most specialized in the world in the area of conscientiology and includes rare volumes. The collection will be able to be accessed through a multimedia data base. This information will eventually be accessible through the world wide web, thus facilitating remote research.

Research

The CEAEC promotes courses in which concepts and research techniques are addressed in order to develop researchers. Research orientation and project development is also offered. Activities include: orientation for laboratorial self-research; development of new laboratories; debates on topics of research. New resources are also developed as forms for registering multidimensional experiences, such as: the Self-researcher's Workbook; Projector's Workbook; Penta Diary. Basic orientation can be received with the "Manual for Developing Research Projects at the CEAEC," which can be downloaded from CEAEC's homepage at www.ceaec.org, or acquired directly from the CEAEC.

Laboratories

CEAEC's laboratories are based on the consciential paradigm, in which the consciousness researches him or herself utilizing projections of the consciousness (OBE) and parapsychic experiences, wherein one is simultaneously the object and subject of research. The laboratories are interdimensional chambers that are technically prepared to optimize consciousness research, supporting the process of self-awareness, development of consciential attributes and the study of multidimensional experiences.

As of August, 1999 the following 9 laboratories are already functioning:

1. Waking Physical Immobility Laboratory.

2. Vibrational State Laboratory.

3. Projective Technique Laboratory (Projectarium).

4. Retrocognition Laboratory (Retrocognitarium).

5. Penta Laboratory.

6. Existential Program Laboratory.

7. Energetic Signaletics Laboratory.

8. Thosenology Laboratory.

9 Self-Organization Laboratory.

Other laboratories are in preparation.

Publications

One of the CEAEC's objectives is to make innovative studies that can enrich the diverse areas of human knowledge and generate opportunities for evolutionary growth of consciousnesses accessible to society, with the dissemination of results from the areas of research proposed by conscientiology. For this reason, the CEAEC produces a diversity of publications, including the CEAEC newsletter, the magazine Conscientia, books, periodicals and collections of articles that allow the exchange of research ideas and the updating of knowledge. Some books already published by the CEAEC are: Our Evolution, Conscientiology Themes, 200 Conscientiology Theorices, 100 Conscientiometric Tests, Consciential Mini-definitions, Nature Instructs (all authored by Dr. Vieira), which deepen the reader's understanding of various aspects of conscientiology. Outlines include The Researcher's Journal, The Projector's Journal, Penta Diary, the CEAEC Research Manual, and Why Iguassu Falls?

Environmental Project

The Environmental Project arose in September of 1995. This mobilized several CEAEC volunteers who were concerned about the environmental impact of the installation of CEAEC on Iguassu Falls city.

Consciential Residential Project - "Field of Dreams"

The Consciential Residential Project serves to catalyze groupal and individual existential programs through high-level work in the area of conviviality that tends to predispose those individuals interested consciousness research to the mega-challenge of unprecedented self-encounter. It takes multidimensionality and the holosomatic process into consideration with the relevant aspects of the conscientiologist's daily life. The project's showroom is a one-bedroom home that is constructed with circular designs. It is an experimental laboratory that represents a break in the existing paradigm of residential construction.

CEAEC Homepage - http://www.ceaec.org

This book researches evolutionology,
which is a field of conscientiology.